Roger Oldcorn is an industrial economist working at Henley – the Management College, where he is Deputy Director of the Management Development and Advisory Service. He worked in the food and hotel industries for several years before joining the Centre for Interfirm Comparison, where he was Senior Projects Manager. He has carried out long-term assignments for the United Nations (UNIDO) in India and the Middle East and also worked as a consultant in the USA. He has been in management education since the mid-1970s and was Business Development Advisor at Kingston Regional Management Centre before moving to Henley. His particular interests include the economic, financial and accounting aspects of corporate planning and business development.

Roger Oldcorn is the author of *Management: A Fresh Approach* and *Understanding Company Accounts* in the Pan Breakthrough series; he is the author of *Company Accounts* in the Pan Management Guides series.

PAN MANAGEMENT GUIDES

Other books in the series:

PAN MANAGEMENT GUIDES

The Management of Business

Roger Oldcorn

A Pan Original
Pan Books London and Sydney

For Howard, Richard
and
Elizabeth

First published 1987 by Pan Books Ltd,
Cavaye Place, London SW10 9PG
9 8 7 6 5 4 3 2 1
© Roger Oldcorn 1987
ISBN 0 330 29776 7
Phototypeset by Input Typesetting Ltd, London SW19 8DR
Printed and bound in Great Britain by
Cox & Wyman Ltd., Reading

Contents

Acknowledgements

The sources of my material are wide and varied. For a start, there are the books and articles quoted in the text, but also there is the experience garnered over many years of dealing with all kinds of business enterprises and all kinds of business managers around the world. In particular, though, I should like to thank all my former and present colleagues at work whose collective wisdom has been a great source of inspiration.

Finally, as ever, if it was not for the support of my family it would have been an impossible task. A million thanks!

Introduction

One of the oldest, and simplest, definitions of 'management' is: 'getting things done through people'. It is not a particularly smart definition but it contains an element of truth. So, if a group of business managers is asked the question: What proportion of your time is spent on people matters and on 'things' or business matters, the answer often averages out at around fifty:fifty, although sometimes there is a bias towards people matters – especially when the firm is going through a bad time.

This book explains the business side of the manager's job; the making sure that things 'get done' efficiently and effectively. It is not about how to recruit, train, motivate and develop people. I believe a firm must decide first what needs to be done – not in a haphazard way, but after great effort and debate – then it must decide how best to accomplish the task.

This book is about what to do in business and how to set about it. One of the problems in writing such a book is the existence of so many types of business organisations, ranging in size from the one-man corner shop, to the multi-national corporation employing thousands. Companies also differ greatly in what they do: from simple retailing (although not as simple as it used to be), to high technology and scientific firms, to the complex financial services world of the City of London.

They are different, yet there are common denominators: they all have money sunk into them; they are all trying to sell something and sell enough to justify the effort, and they are all trying to operate efficiently and make sure that the amount of money going out is less than the amount of money coming in. These common denominators make it possible to set out principles of good business practice – and it is these principles that are addressed in this book.

We will consider:

- Setting objectives,
- analysing the firm and its environment,
- strategy formulation,
- establishing policies (or operating rules) in different functions of the firm, and
- keeping things under control.

Generally, the book looks at business through the eyes of senior management: those people who have overall responsibility for the firm and its survival; this applies to small firms as well as large firms.

Departmental managers working in large organisations may feel some of the subject matter is either irrelevant, or that they are incapable of doing anything about it. They may feel: 'I cannot do anything about the corporate strategy of the company . . . if I said anything I would be told to never mind all that, just get on with your job'. My answer is that all managers are welcome to take the least line of resistance and not stir things up. However, successful managers do ask questions of their senior managers and make suggestions for improvement.

As far as irrelevance is concerned, remember E. M. Forster's phrase in Howard's End: 'Only connect'. In other words, try to connect the ideas in the book with your own situation and ask: 'How can I apply this notion to my own area of responsibility to make it more effective?'

The job of the manager in business offers great challenges and great opportunities. However, the opportunities will not turn into anything material if the manager simply concentrates on today's problems without giving a thought as to where he is heading. It is too easy to focus on the things we know and to deal with the immediate needs of the job. Time must be taken to think about where you are heading and this book should help start this process. It should raise lots of questions in your mind and, hopefully, you will want to follow up some of the ideas – the reading list at the end will help. There is plenty of literature on management in business and new ideas appear weekly. It really is worthwhile setting aside a little time each week to read about business management, and to think how to apply the best ideas to your own situation. There will be a payoff one day!

1 What is Management in Business?

What exactly is involved in being a business manager and what makes that kind of work different from other jobs? For an answer consider this description of a business manager's job, given by the manager himself:

> I run a supermarket. I do not own the shop, I was simply put in charge of it by the owners who have a chain of similar shops up and down the country. My title is 'Store Manager' to identify me as the man in charge.
>
> 'At first I thought my job was to sell goods, but I soon discovered that was merely a means to an end – the end being to make a profit. In fact, my job is exactly the same as the job of top managers in the biggest firms in the land – the only differences being in size and in the number of people to help me. I'm a very busy businessman and my job is to make sure the shop makes a profit – and more profit this year than last year.

This statement describes that particular manager's overall responsibilities, but it tells us very little about what he actually does. If we questioned him further and asked him how he makes sure that the shop makes a profit, he might answer like this:

> Every day I have to make sure the shop is open on time and that it is clean, tidy and looks inviting. I have to be sure that the staff are clean and tidy too, and in a reasonably good mood. It is very important to make sure that we have the right number of trained

staff available and that there is proper cover for holidays. I have also to deal with customer complaints and many telephone calls. I have to make sure that all repairs and maintenance are carried out quickly and properly. If I want to make major alterations to the shop I have to seek head office approval – and to be sure of getting the approval I have to argue my case well and that involves a lot of preparation. It's the same thing if I want to hire extra staff. My main concern is making sure that the shelves are always properly filled with the right kind of goods. I have to decide what to order and where to position goods.

There are many other duties – ensuring that the till money is correct and banked, reading all the paper that comes in, dealing with health and safety matters and preventing theft. My assistants help me in many of these things, but at the end of the day it is my responsibility to see that everything is running smoothly. The really important piece of paper I receive each week is the accounting report from head office. This shows our turnover and profit; it tells us how we're doing and keeps us all on our toes.

It is not difficult to see why this manager sees himself as a busy businessman. It is not quite so easy to see why he is called a manager. If we think about the tasks he mentioned, some could be done by anyone – the manager is responsible overall but can delegate the work to others. Some duties, though, are his sole responsibility and these are the hallmarks of management. For instance, to ensure that the shop opens on time is a straightforward job; it is the manager's responsibility but he can easily get someone else to do it for him because no decisions are involved. On the other hand, the problems of ordering many different types of products and deciding how to position them on the shelves require judgement. These decisions will significantly affect the profit of the shop. That area is the manager's own. Similarly, staff matters are tasks the manager has to handle himself; he is paid to make sure the staff work efficiently and with enthusiasm.

It is easy to see that this manager is a business 'manager'; his title is 'Manager' and the nature of his job indicates he has responsibilities of a managerial nature and is working in a business environment. In business many thousands of people are called 'manager' and, generally, they are given the title because they have, like the supermarket manager, these special responsibilities. Many people, though, are business managers even if they do not carry the title: executive and director being the most common. Indeed an engineer, an accountant and anyone running their own business can be described as a business manager. The range of jobs covered by the phrase 'business manager' is therefore huge. The skills needed vary from business to business: the local butcher and the computer expert running a small computer software house are both business managers in entirely different worlds.

They are all described as business managers because they all have managerial responsibilities like those of the supermarket manager. So what are these responsibilities and how do you know if a particular job carries them? Is it possible to identify if someone is a business manager simply by finding out what his job consists of? The answer becomes clearer if you look at the jobs pages in the papers.

Consider the following extracts from real advertisements that have appeared in the paper. You will find, as you read them, that the same words – or similar – crop up again and again. These are the common threads which describe the job of management.

1 *Managing Director:* . . . who has had both production

and managerial responsibility to take over the financial, commercial and industrial relations activities of the operations. The appointment is to substantially increase production and profits.

2 *Assistant General Manager:* . . . to manage and control the various service sections of head office. Major elements of the job are industrial relations and in-company communications. He will also deputise for the General Manager.

3 *Research & Development Manager:* . . . to take over an existing successful R & D section and build it up to a department of about twenty scientists, responsible for carrying out projects worldwide. Will have to be a talented leader with entrepreneurial skills.

4 *Production Planning Manager:* . . . involves the programming of current production and its control using computer systems to monitor and record production activity. Will also advise the Production Director on means of expanding the facilities to meet future growth.

5 *Marketing Manager:* . . . you will plan all marketing activities, liaise with sister overseas firms, plan new product launch, gather market intelligence, control all promotional activities, assist in the development of corporate plans.

6 *Marketing Manager:* . . . responsibility will encompass all aspects of business development from the creation of marketing and advertising plans to the motivation and control of distributors in the field.

7 *Distribution Manager:* . . . you will have responsibility for the overall control of the warehousing and distribution in the UK. You will manage the resources to ensure the efficient delivery of products into stock locations and distribution to retail outlets.

8 *Personnel Manager:* . . . will have overall responsibility for all personnel functions with particular emphasis on industrial relations. Negotiating skills are essential together with an ability to react quickly to changing circumstances.

9 *Manager Production Control:* . . . wide-ranging responsibilities including devising monthly production plans, coordinating regular checks on stock levels, maintaining first-class communications between production and sales.

These job descriptions cover different managerial jobs. Yet even though the work may differ greatly there are common elements running through most, if not all, of the descriptions – even to the extent that the same words crop up again and again.

Some of the words quoted need special mention; one of them is *'leader'*, a word which suggests an army officer going into battle first and getting his men to rally round him and charge. In that sense the word might not be all that suitable for a modern manager inside a big civil organisation, although all managers have to be 'out in front' some of the time. 'Leading' in another sense means 'direct the movements of', and where a manager has staff responsibilities the role of leader becomes meaningful in this context and indeed a manager with responsibilities for materials or services may have to direct their movement too.

Another word used directly related to leading, so far as people is concerned, is *'motivate'*. It is interesting that only one of the nine uses this word, yet at least six or seven have staff responsibilities. Why is it not mentioned? Is it because it is not thought to be important? Or is it because it is assumed that it is automatically part of the job?

'Industrial relations' are two words that also seem to

crop up from time to time and suggest an area of concern for managers generally. This again is associated with motivation and leadership and revolves around the whole question of people at work.

'*Planning*' crops up several times and is implicit in all cases. It can obviously be assumed in the case of the managing director; the assistant general managers and personnel managers will certainly have to do some planning.

'*Control*' is spelt out in five cases. However, the four managers who do not have the word in the description of their jobs are most likely to be in control of something. The word responsibility is contained in each of these four managers' job descriptions and that alone suggests that control is an integral part of the job of being responsible for something.

'*Financial responsibilities*' only appears once (the managing director). However we can assume that all have some financial responsibilities, because all have responsibility for a part of the business that spends money.

The word '*communications*' is specially mentioned in some of the job descriptions, but this is not to imply that the other managers do not have to communicate. Indeed, reading between the lines, it is clear that managerial responsibility must include a great deal of communicating.

Other key words that occur and which are worth noting as describing the job of management are:

- *negotiating*
- *leading*
- *motivating*
- *creating*
- *coordinating*
- *entrepreneurial skills*

One aspect of most of these managers' jobs which is

not usually spelt out clearly is that of responsibility for staff. Some of the managers will obviously have people reporting to them, for example the two marketing managers, but for the manager of production control (No. 9) and the production planning manager (No. 4) there is no indication of staff responsibilities at all.

Finally, a missing phrase which is integral to all management jobs is that of decision-making. For instance all the managers with staff responsibilities will have to take decisions about their staff. All the managers responsible for seeing that something is done will have to make decisions. 'Ensure the efficient delivery of products' is the kind of responsibility that can only be effective if a decision-making power is included. Some are much more involved with communications than others and this can be seen from the descriptions of their duties, but it is rare for any manager to have no regular need to communicate 'sideways'.

What emerges from the nine job descriptions is a composite picture of the business manager's job. It involves a fair proportion of planning the activities for which he is responsible. It also involves keeping these activities under control. Many managers have staff responsibilities, have to motivate staff and guide them and sometimes become involved in industrial relations matters. Many have a financial concern as part of their area of responsibility. All managers have to communicate and also take decisions.

In addition to all these specifically managerial skills the managers are, of course, experts in their own chosen fields – as production people, marketing men or just complete businessmen.

Another look at the job of management

One of the first persons to sit down and try to work out what managers do (and what they should do) was a Frenchman called Henri Fayol. Fayol was a mining engineer who became managing director of an ailing coalmining firm and turned it into a highly successful coal and steel business. All this took place between 1888 and 1918, when he retired. In 1916, after many years thinking about the job of the manager, he published a small book called *General and Industrial Management*. Oddly enough it was years before a translation appeared in English, even though it contains a great deal of wisdom and sense. Part of the book deals with the 'elements' or 'functions' of management, and Fayol identifies five such functions. They are:

- *Planning*
- *Organising*
- *Command*
- *Coordination*
- *Control*

It is important to appreciate what Fayol meant by these five functions:

- *Planning* is looking ahead and making provision for the future. Failure to plan signifies managerial incompetence.
- *Organising* is providing the business with everything it needs to operate (equipment, materials, finance, people) and includes management training as a key part in it.
- *Command* is how organising gets achieved; in a nutshell it is directing subordinates.
- *Coordination* is harmonising activities for successful results.

- *Control* is making sure things happen the way they were planned.

The first and last functions – planning and control – are immediately recognisable from the analysis that we have carried out, and there tends to be less argument about these two functions than about the others.

Organising is, of course, similar to planning in that it is concerned with preparation for some future events. But whereas planning is the more glamorous activity of deciding on the overall future direction of the business, organising is that tough, demanding activity of putting together the elements in such a way that the overall plans actually succeed.

Command is seen as the function that actually makes things happen. It is really derived from military practice, and no doubt in Fayol's time all employees in companies responded to command. The very word suggests 'ordering about'. Fayol did not really intend it to be taken in a very narrow sense, but rather in the sense of making sure that things get done – the actual operations of the company. As a result, many substitute words have been used, like 'direction' and even 'actuating'.

The fifth function of management, in Fayol's view, is that of coordination. It requires harmony, making sure that all the bits work together and, like an orchestra under its conductor, play the same tune. This is the only function that does not seem easily to stand on its own and will be found to be part of planning, of organising, of control and the key to successful operations themselves.

Scientific management

Although the ideas of Henri Fayol have been taken on
board by many writers and practitioners of management in the last twenty-five to thirty years, earlier
management theory depended for its main prop on the
writings of an American engineer called Frederick W.
Taylor. In his work at the Midvale Steel Company in
Philadelphia (from 1884 he was the chief engineer), he
tried to apply scientific and engineering principles to
the work of people (in those days steelmaking was
highly labour intensive). He decided that there was one
best way to do things and he sought to find it. In
1911 he published his book *The Principles of Scientific
Management*, which is concerned mainly with explaining
how a scientific approach to work could reduce stress
and wear and tear on people, at the same time
improving output. Taylor was the original 'time and
motion' man. In addition he stressed such factors as
planning work, getting work organised and training
staff, all as part of the responsibilities of management.

Since those days a vast amount has been written
about what management is, what it should be and what
it does. Some of these writers will be introduced as
appropriate during the detailed discussions to follow.
Suffice it to say that the broad functions of planning,
organising, doing the job and control have all been
studied, researched and analysed extensively.

What should managers do?

Taking the four functions of management just
described, one of the most fascinating games to play is
to try to calculate how managers should spend their
time and how they actually do spend their time. In
theory the most senior managers in an organisation

should spend most of their time planning, some time organising, some controlling and very little actually doing the work.

In contrast, middle management's job is mainly concerned with organising and control, a little on planning and some actual work. At least, it sounds right.

'First-line' managers, finally, are mainly concerned with control and doing the job, and only a very small proportion of their time should be spent planning and organising.

Research carried out during the last twenty years or so has revealed very interesting things about what managers actually do. It seems that lower levels of management spend most of their time 'doing the job'. Middle and senior managers, it seems, spend far more time 'doing' than planning, organising and controlling.

The supermarket manager we looked at early in the chapter could classify his work in the terminology of Henri Fayol:

- Planning (ordering stock, staffing).
- Organising (making sure the store can actually function properly).
- Control (keeping his eye on things, people and money).
- Doing the job.

The store manager called himself a very busy businessman; he might have called himself a busy manager, which he most certainly was. To do his job effectively he had to possess a remarkably wide range of knowledge, skills and abilities:

- Knowledge about the retailing, the products sold, retail shop matters, the company, the town.
- Skills relating to taking decisions, communicating, handling people, selling.
- Ability to plan, organise, control.

The whole range of activities seems formidable yet is not unusual. All managers have to know about the type of work they are doing – the 'knowledge' aspects of the job. In addition, there are all the skills and abilities. It does not seem possible that any one individual could excel at all these different activities. Indeed there are very few managers who could even be described as 'pretty good' at most things. These people are often found at the top of companies – not necessarily the managing director, but certainly heading up a major function.

For all the other managers, the aim is to try to be as effective as possible in as many ways as possible. Ultimately it is the manager who is in charge, who is responsible for the success of the activities entrusted to him.

The view from the top

All managers who have overall responsibilities for a business, whether it be a one-man outfit, a small firm or a subsidiary of a multinational corporation, tend to view their work differently from that of a junior or middle manager. The case that follows highlights the type of task being handled at each stage. The key words are set out alongside the text on the right of the page.

SPRINKLO LTD

Sprinklo had a problem. It manufactured and sold a range of plastic watering-cans throughout Britain. The profits were barely adequate and there was little foreseeable growth in the UK market. It was decided that the firm should be aiming to double its profits within four years.

  A great deal of analysis took place – it was found that there was plenty of spare capacity in the factory and that the European market was underdeveloped.

  It was decided to sell the products in W. Germany and as a first step a small task force was sent out to set up a marketing operation over there. As a result the whole company was reorganised with an export sales and distribution office and the creation of a German subsidiary.

  Some important decisions were taken at this stage – no advertising on TV, but a large sales force would cover the main markets. The product would be made in Britain but shipped to Germany monthly and held in store against orders. The German operation had to be self-funding after four months.

  The target sales for the first year were set, salesmen were hired and trained, and each was given a territory to cover. On the first of January the team started work and at first, at the end of each day, the salesmen phoned the German sales manager giving details of the number of orders he had obtained.

  In turn, the German sales office kept the UK office informed of progress and a close check was kept on

SETTING
OBJECTIVES
ANALYSIS OF
STRENGTHS AND
WEAKNESSES:
ENVIRONMENTAL
THREATS AND
OPPORTUNITIES
(SWOT)
STRATEGY
STRUCTURE

POLICIES

OPERATIONS
PLANNING

OPERATIONS

CONTROL

the quantities being moved out of CONTROL
the warehouse.

At the end of the first year, the
managing director of Sprinklo was
able to inform the shareholders that
the company was well on course to
meeting its objectives.

This case example puts a different perspective on the
job of the business manager to that of the supermarket
manager yet the same words crop up and the same
functions are taking place. In the chapters that follow
the topics named above will be examined in detail so
that all managers in business can see how their job ties
in with the overall corporate aims and policies.

2 Planning: Aims and Objectives in Business

The first task of the manager is to make sure that the activities for which he is responsible are successful. Unfortunately, merely working hard does not guarantee success; in addition there should be a lot of thinking about the future, and the first step in this process is to set aims and objectives for that area of responsibility. The importance of objectives can easily be demonstrated: imagine what would happen if, when you caught your bus in the morning, the conductor told you the bus was going to the cemetery instead of the railway station as you had expected. Suppose, then, that some of the other passengers thought the bus was going to the town hall and others believed it was heading for the hospital. Sooner or later, the driver would have to be consulted, and he could do one of several things, none of which would be entirely satisfactory. The situation could have been avoided if the destination of the bus had been settled at the outset and arose even though only one manager was involved (the driver of the bus). In many situations more than one manager is involved and so it takes even longer to arrive at a decision. It would be like two small boys in a rowing boat on a boating pond each with one oar: a lot of energy, noise and aggravation, but little progress of any significance.

These simple examples show that without some clear idea of destination things will not turn out well, and this is as true for any organisation as it is for a bus or a rowing boat. It should be possible to ask of any organisation, Where is it going? Or, more accurately,

What is the aim or purpose of this organisation? Unfortunately, the answer may not be as clearly stated as the question.

In one sense, however, all companies limited under the Companies Acts have their aims written down in what is usually referred to as the 'objects clause' in the firm's memorandum of association. The objects clause is a legal requirement and is constructed in such a way as to enable the company to do almost whatever it wants. Bearing in mind that the legal objectives of a company are established when the firm itself comes into being, it is quite likely that the words bear little relevance today for the company that is old-established.

Our concern here is with objectives that help the management of the organisation in its day-to-day running of the business. Clearly stated, objectives should provide the reference point around which all decisions affecting the future of the organisation can be taken. Without the objectives, the organisation is like the rowing boat full of little boys – except that nothing much is lost if the boys get nowhere, but an organisation which fails can be the cause of great hardship.

It is important to recognise that objectives may refer to something in the fairly near future or may be an expression of some wish that may take years to achieve (if ever). For instance, at the beginning of every football season the members, players and fans of every football club in the land will set out a whole series of objectives, which will range from winning the first match of the season to winning the league title or some cup competition during the coming months. The more avid fans will dream of great success like winning the European Cup, and the manager will dream of being rich and famous, because his club is rich and successful. For some clubs these dreams may be close at hand; for most, though, they are likely to be pipe-dreams only.

It is also important to realise that objectives can be

set for the company as a whole and are usually called 'corporate objectives'. In addition, however, each recognisable part of the company will also have its own objectives. These will be known as 'departmental', 'divisional', 'branch' or 'project' objectives depending on how the company is split up. Finally, all the individuals in the company should have their own objectives (in relation to the company). These will be set out in the employee's job description, or at least should be.

Unfortunately, objectives are often not clearly set out at any level in the company. Not only should they be made explicit, but they should all point in the same direction. For example, it is dangerous to have the buying department's objective as 'to buy as cheaply as possible' while at the same time expecting the production department to have an objective which includes minimising waste. If this were the case the buyers would buy the cheapest materials on the market, but in doing so they would possibly be buying materials at a quality too low for satisfactory production. This would lead to a high wastage level and the failure of the production department to meet its own objectives. Individual and departmental objectives have to be in line with each other and have to agree also with the overall objectives of the company.

What is needed therefore is a set of objectives for a company and its parts which are in harmony with each other: objectives which will guide the company's actions over a reasonable period of time. The key question to be answered is, What might reasonable corporate objectives be?

The answer to this question obviously depends on the company – its size and the nature of its activities. The more complex the organisation, the more difficult it is to come up with answers that have any real meaning. Even in the smallest, simplest company the answer to the question What are the objectives? is not necessarily as easy as it might seem. Take for instance the case of a major in the army retiring at the age of fifty who decides to go into business on his own. He has a pension and a gratuity and he could afford to do nothing for the rest of his life if he invested the gratuity wisely. Instead he chooses to use the gratuity to buy a small business – a pub, newsagent's shop or sub-post-office being among the favourites. His reasons for going into business on his own usually start with a very strong desire not to rot quietly away in retirement. The second reason is an equally strong desire to be his own master for a change, instead of living under strict rules, regulations and orders. From this point on the reasons tend to be financial, and while there are some who adopt a 'get rich quick' approach, the majority of people in these circumstances will have an aim that can be described like this:

I want the business to be able to give me a lifestyle I should like to be accustomed to, and at the same time enable me to sell up in ten years' time having made my gratuity grow in real terms over the period (i.e. faster than inflation).

There is in this statement a potential conflict that all would-be small business owners have to guard against, namely that it is easy to take out of the business enough to give one a good living, but this may lead to starving the business of the funds it needs to grow and become of greater value.

It will be noticed that at this stage no mention has been made of the type of business the retiring officer wants to invest in. The reason appears to be that someone who goes through the rationalising process just described ends up choosing a business that is most likely to satisfy his requirements, irrespective of what the business might be. On the other hand there are some who enter a particular type of business because they have always had an ambition to do so. Many famous companies began in this way. Sainsbury's the supermarket chain began as a small grocer's shop in London's Drury Lane. The Beecham Group – world famous for its pharmaceuticals as well as for Macleans toothpaste, Ribena and many other household products – began with Mr Beecham selling his pills in market places up and down the land.

So for the one-man operation there appears to be no problem; the owner/manager sets the objectives and these are fairly clear-cut and obvious. But what about in larger organisations? What are the objectives of a large company like ICI which has thousands of shareholders (who are legally the owners of the business)? The objectives we used for the small business cannot be suitable for the big firm. What we need are objectives which make sense for companies where the managers and the owners may well be different people. Here are some of the most commonly found corporate objectives:

1 Survive

Unless a company is set up with a specific task in mind, and is folded up on completion of that job, it can be fairly assumed that all companies (and indeed all parts of all companies) want to survive. To be more specific, the individuals involved in the affairs of the unit or company do not want to see their jobs disappear (unless they are, Samson-like, deliberately planning self-destruction too). It is, therefore, a minimum requirement that organisations should survive, with no limits set on their lifespan. Generally, the threat of extinction concentrates management's mind, and that of all employees, more effectively than most other situations. It is worth reminding one's colleagues from time to time that, no matter how successfully everything is going now, something could be just around the corner

˙ʋ damage or destroy the set-up. This applies to departments or groups within organisations even more than it applies to whole outfits, and the event has to be avoided.

2 *Provide a service*

This kind of objective is to be found mainly in non-commercial organisations, which do not have the yardstick of profit to consider but which are set up primarily for some social purpose. This is not to imply that they do not have to consider financial issues – indeed many social institutions are primarily concerned with money. However, money for such institutions is regarded as the means to the end – the end being effective performance of the service itself. In contrast, insurance companies and building societies all provide specific and valuable services to the community as a whole. The same is true of banks and many other organisations that provide professional or technical services, from estate agents to petrol stations. No doubt the services they provide are included in their objectives, but it is a matter of some debate as to whether they would regard 'provision of the service' as their primary objective.

Firms manufacturing useful products to many different end-users are also providing a service by making available their products and satisfying certain requirements of the market. Again, the service provided can be an objective, but whether it is the main objective is debatable.

3 *Grow*

Many organisations have an ambition to grow, but growth itself has little merit as an objective unless it is a clear idea of what it is that has to be grown. Many commercial organisations regard growth of the share of the market as a critically important objective. Others see a rise in market share as a means to achieving what they think are much more important objectives – growth in profits or in the size of the firm.

Growth is the objective of the ambitious and it can refer to the owner of a shop who wants to open another branch, or to the biggest firm in the world. Many large companies aim to make sales grow at least as fast as the growth in the economy of the country as a whole. The reasons for this kind of attitude are that real growth gives short-term tangible benefits in terms of profits, everyone is kept busy and it feels good to be part of a growing concern.

However, some companies have no desire to grow, particularly where ownership is in the hands of an individual or family. There comes a point where to achieve any further growth in the business requires more money than can be raised or borrowed by the family; the only thing to do would be to offer outsiders shares in the firm and this would lead ultimately to the family not having a majority of the shares. Thus they would lose control of the firm. Effective control can also be lost if a business grows to the extent that the owner has to appoint, for the first time, managers. Many owners do not want this to happen and prefer to stay small.

4 Be big

To have an objective that includes being big automatically must also have growth in mind. Growth, then, becomes not an objective in itself, but a way in which the objective of size is to be achieved. There are several ways in which size can be measured.

■ The value of external sales is popular since it does

reflect the extent to which a company has penetrated the markets it is serving.

- The size of the firm's profits (before or after tax has been deducted).
- The total value of the firm's assets (its land, buildings, machinery, stocks, investments, cash in the bank and so on).
- The 'net worth' of the business (the value of assets less the amount borrowed; sometimes called equity capital).
- The 'market value' of the firm (only possible if the firm is quoted on the stock market. It is the value of the shares in total at a point in time).
- Other measures used are purely physical units – like the number of employees. Particular industries have their own favourite measures; the airlines use passenger miles, road haulage uses ton miles, and the paint industry will use gallons (or litres) of paint.

Finally, as regards being big, there are two major disadvantages. First, being large attracts a lot of attention, especially from groups who have legal, social or moral objections to such size. This includes the Monopolies Commission and from time to time (depending on the policies of the government in office) various prices control boards. Second, being large is no guarantee of survival or prosperity. Economists often write about 'economies of scale'. This means simply that if an operation is big, it can buy cheaper, make more efficiently and sell at lower cost than the smaller operator. These savings help the larger to make more profit and, if this profit is used wisely, the firm should have a better chance of survival than if it was small. Unfortunately, the evidence does not always support this theory. Many large firms have failed to survive and many fail to make even modest levels of profit. Size is no guarantee of success.

5 Be efficient

Efficiency on its own is not usually regarded as the primary objective of companies, but rather as an essential ingredient with other objectives. For instance, a building society's objective may be 'to collect and distribute money efficiently'; a builder may have the objective of 'efficient house-construction'. Only two things need to be said about efficiency; first, no company, or part of a company, is 100 per cent efficient. There is always room for improvement and so efficiency should always be built into objectives. Second, there is no point in being efficient if nobody is interested in the results anyway. It is of no help to a maker of slide-rules that they are manufactured efficiently, when there is very little demand for them.

Efficiency and effectiveness
I see 'efficiency' as being concerned to do things rightly – perhaps overlooking the fact that one is spending time and effort doing right and well things that ought not to be done at all! The people who spend considerable amounts of time and effort doing a little more efficiently what should not be done at all are the bane of my life . . . Effectiveness is doing the right things

Peter Drucker
(in a talk to the British Institute of Management 1964)

If, however, efficiency is deliberately ignored, *inefficiency* is being condoned and that cannot be good. The requirement for a good objective is that it combines the need for efficiency with the need to do things right. Very often they are brought together under the specifically financial objectives of 'profit' and 'profitability'.

6 Make a profit

Profits can be made only when something is sold or hired out. The important point about 'profit' is that failure to achieve it threatens the survival of every commercial undertaking.

The advantage of a financial objective, like profit, is that it can be turned into a number, and it is very easy to compare a number objective with the actual result – also expressed as a number. So if a company wants a profit of £1 million next year and only achieves £900 thousand, it is easy to see that it has failed to meet its objective. When specific numbers are attached to objectives in this way, it is usual to refer to them as 'Goals'. In other words they are specific targets to aim at. Most companies include the word 'profit' in their statement of objectives. Unfortunately, on its own, profit is a meaningless statement because there are several different types of profit which can be very different in size, depending on whether such things as corporation tax have been included*.

Profit measures are useful targets to aim at, but they do not lend themselves to comparison – mainly because inflation distorts the value of money over time. Moreover, to have as an objective 'to make a profit' is a bit simple: £1 would meet the objective. In the old days economists used to write that firms existed to 'maximise' profit. The problems with this concept are that it is impossible to put a figure on it, it assumes a very short lifespan for the firm concerned and it fails to recognise that maximising profit one year could spoil the profits in the long run. To make an adequate profit is a better objective, but this leaves the problem of defining 'adequate', which is where the objective of profitability is helpful.

* For a more detailed explanation of this see *Company Accounts* by Roger Oldcorn in the Pan Management Guides series.

7 Be profitable

If you put £100 into a building society for a year and receive interest of £10 at the end of the year, the return on your investment is ten per cent. Similarly if you were a rich shipping magnate and spent £100 million on some new boats which brought in a profit of £10 million (after tax), your return on investment would be ten per cent also. In both cases the equation can be called profitability; it is an expression of the successful use of the basic resources of the business – money and people. All businesses are the same in this respect: money is put in and used by people to obtain facilities, equipment and other resources which are used by people to produce and sell goods and services. The activities should yield a money surplus if the operation has been well run. If badly run, there is no surplus, no profit and ultimately the firm expires. To put £100 in and get £25 out each year is very different to only getting £2 out. Not only is the £2 result less profitable; the firm has been less efficient. The more we get out the more profitable we are.

Precisely how to measure profitability is open to argument, and which measure to use as an objective is also arguable.

In the United States it is common to refer to 'earnings per share' (EPS) as the key criterion of a firm's success*, and most companies have this item quantified as a long-term objective. Many writers refer to 'return on investment' or 'return on capital employed' or 'return on equity' as the most suitable financial objective (usually abbreviated to ROI, ROCE or ROE). In Britain, company accounts more often than not show EPS and often another measure of profitability as well.

---

* 'Earnings' being another word for profit after tax and interest payments have been deducted.

8 Satisfy the owners

If a company is very profitable, it can give the share-holders a good return on their investment and plough back a lot of money into the business. This enables it to grow and make even bigger profits so it can give the shareholders an even better return on their investment, and so on. The shareholders might well be described as being relatively well satisfied with the company. But is it enough just to have as a basic objective 'to satisfy the owners'?

The answer depends on what the people inside the company, who set the objectives in the first place, think. In turn, what they think depends on their attitudes and beliefs. If, however, it is not enough to merely satisfy the shareholders, for whom does a company exist? Who is it there to satisfy? There are several possibilities:

Possibility 1 – the shareholders. This is the traditional view. The owners of the organisation invest (or really risk) their money in the business and, as long as they get a decent return, the company has fulfilled its purpose. This view is supported by reference to many clubs and societies – the local bowls club exists to satisfy its members and that is all.

Possibility 2 – the customers. As long as an organisation satisfies its customers then it has met its primary purpose. Certainly if it does not it will not survive for very long. Respectable organisations try to resist the image of the fly-by-night operator: the firm that sells a dud product and disappears. Moreover there is a tendency for firms to exercise a greater degree of responsibility in the goods and services they sell and the way they are sold.

Possibility 3 – the employees. Instead of regarding people as just another raw material to be exploited, many companies consider that trying to satisfy employees is a key aim. The equations are:

- Dissatisfied employees = low productivity, trouble, strikes.
- Satisfied employees = high productivity, peace, prosperity.

Contrast this with the Dickensian image of lower wages = higher profits for owners.

Possibility 4 – management. Managers are employees too, and also may be shareholders and customers. The view is that because managers are the people with the power inside organisations (they make the decisions), they are the people who want to be satisfied most. The organisation exists for them; not just 'top management' but all managers. John Kenneth Galbraith talks about the real control being in the hands of the 'technocrats' – those who have the skills and expertise within the organisation to be able to run it.

Possibility 5 – everyone involved. Why not try to satisfy everyone involved in the firm? Not just shareholders, managers, employees and customers, but the whole community whose lives are one way or another affected by the organisation and its presence. The word 'stake-holder' has been used to describe all these different people, and there is a growing body of opinion to support the idea that organisations must seek to satisfy all the stakeholders.

Failure to keep any one group happy can lead to trouble. Avoiding trouble is a highly practical reason for trying to satisfy all the stakeholders, but there is a more powerful reason: that all organisations exist in society and must behave responsibly towards it. The suggestion is that they have a duty, beyond what is required by law or forced on them by pressure groups. To quote Peter Drucker again: 'the business enterprise has to add to its fundamental concern for the quantities of life (economic goods and services) a concern for the quality of life, for the physical, human and social environment of modern men and modern community'.

So there are two extremes:

- On one hand the objective is high profits to satisfy the shareholders – the other stakeholders and matters of social responsibility are factors which contribute to the main purpose.
- In contrast, the objective is to be socially responsible by satisfying all the stakeholders.

The argument is brilliantly set out as far as banks are concerned in the novel by Arthur Hailey *The Money Changers* (Part 1, Chapter 15)*. Two candidates for the presidency of an American bank each make a presentation to the board of directors of the bank in support of their claim. Both speak of the role of the bank, what it is and what it should be. However, one of the candidates states that profit is their principal objective, and they do not achieve maximum profit by becoming involved in various social issues such as loans to minority groups, housing projects, environmental matters. The other candidate, while reaffirming his own belief in profitability, goes on to assert that new standards are being demanded of industry and business so that the name of the game is 'corporate social responsibility'. In effect, the suggestion is that social responsibility is every bit as important as profit for the second speaker. Although this is a fictional debate, it is not untypical of the arguments that have been and are taking place in relation to commercial organisations generally.

* Pan Books, 1976.

All this gives us at least three more possible corporate objectives:

9 *Satisfy the shareholders*

10 *Satisfy the staff*

11 *Satisfy all the stakeholders*

Consider now three real comments:

Three views of corporate aims, objectives and responsibilities

Three well-known British companies are quoted below. The statements have been made publicly either in annual reports or quoted in the press.

FISONS LTD*.

The objective is consistently to achieve profitable growth in real terms by increasing earnings per share and raising the return on capital employed . . . A leading question . . . was the relative priority between financial and non-financial objectives. What should managers choose today – social responsibility or earnings per share? Could the primary objective of a publicly quoted company be non-financial? I think not. We are surrounded by voices telling us that it can and must: but I think it cannot and must not.

A company had three available resources – raw materials, people and capital – and it could survive only by using them efficiently. Job satisfaction, employee

* Quoted in the *Financial Times*, 12 April 1977, on a paper by Dr Heinz Redwood, formerly general manager of corporate planning, Fisons.

participation, social responsibility and environmental concern were important matters in their own right and also as constraints against making financial objectives the only factor.

At the same time, the financially successful company had a better chance of complying with society's demands and satisfying the aspirations of its employees than one that was forever grappling with a cash crisis . . . the objective best served and safeguarded the company's employees and the external business partners.

MARKS & SPENCER LTD*

We need adequate profits:

1 to maintain and improve the quality of our merchandise, service and stores;
2 for our store development programme in the UK which will cost £300,000,000 over the next four years;
3 to reward the 260,000 shareholders, who include major insurance companies and pension funds, and many small holders, including nearly half our staff;
4 to reward our staff;
5 to take care of our pensioners.

We recognize our social responsibilities and help the communities in which our customers and staff live. We shall make progress so long as we pay attention to people, and continue to be sensitive to the needs of our customers.

* Extracts from the Chairman's Statement (The Hon. Sir Marcus Sieff) in the 1979 Accounts.

Tesco Stores Ltd*

He [the late Sir John Cohen, founder of the Tesco Group] instilled in the whole organisation the total importance of the customer to us, the people who matter are our customers, our shareholders and our staff. We feel that, if we are single-minded in looking after these three groups we have done our job.

One question which remains to be answered is, Who sets corporate objectives? If we support the view that the shareholders (or owners) are the only beneficiaries of a firm, they set the objectives. If, however, we think that all the stakeholders have to be satisfied, presumably there has to be a consensus – everyone involved has to agree on how the cake should be cut. This is impractical; in fact it is top management that decides whether 'top managers' are shareholders or not. What they choose as objectives depends, as we suggested, on their attitudes and beliefs. Business concerns, especially if small, are often run for the benefit of the owner, with other stakeholders and social responsibilities acting as constraints. Large firms recognise the need to look after many stakeholders, even though this can mean a lot of compromise.

Departmental aims

At the start of the chapter we saw that, within a company, the different departments and activities all should have their own objectives. Sometimes it is not easy for a manager to define his own department's objectives, especially where the department exists as a service function to the company as a whole. Beyond

* Statement made by former Tesco Chairman Sir Leslie Porter and quoted in *Checkout* a paper published for shareholders and employees of Tesco (July 1979)

basic survival and 'provide a service', typical objectives might include such things as:

- provide an efficient service
- reduce the cost of the service
- increase the speed or reliability of the service
- develop the function to give a wider service.

As soon as departmental objectives are established, it is easy for individuals to have their own work objectives.

A final word on aims

Sometimes there is confusion about the words used when the talk is about aims and objectives. This can be avoided if the three levels are remembered:

- the general statement of aim – can be called purpose or mission
- the precise things that are being aimed at – the objectives themselves
- the actual numbers being aimed at – the target or goal.

Remember also that there can be a primary or major objective and several secondary or supporting objectives. It is a mistake to think that objectives have to be stated in just a few words – take as many as you like; everyone concerned must not only be able to see them, but they must be able to understand them, as well.

3 Planning: Analysing Strengths and Weaknesses

An essential part of the business planning process is to identify the strengths and weaknesses of the firm. The reason is simple: *strong points* in a business have to be maintained and form the basis for developing the firm. In contrast a *weakness* has to be avoided if at all possible: one must not depend on a weak link and ideally it should be cured. Successful companies have learned this lesson; failures have ignored it. This is not the whole story, though. Corporate success or failure may result from factors outside the company's control. For instance, a shop could find that an increase in tax doubles the price of the goods it is selling. Its prospects would be somewhat reduced through no fault of its own. These external influences on performance will be dealt with in Chapter 4. For now, our attention must be on factors within the firm that are under its control and which have caused it to be successful or not. No company is entirely free of weaknesses, just as no firm is entirely without strong points. Even the biggest failure in the land has something to be said in its favour. The hard part is actually identifying the 'good' parts and distinguishing them from the areas of weakness.

How to identify strengths and weaknesses

Suppose that one Sunday morning you are chatting to your neighbour and you casually mention that you have a touch of toothache. Before you know where you are, he has you tied to a chair in the kitchen and is pulling away on one of your teeth with a pair of pliers. Unless the neighbour happens to be a dentist who is completely up to date on the state of your teeth it is highly unlikely that such an event would take place. Why? For at least two reasons. First, because no amateur would attempt to identify and remove another adult's tooth except in an emergency. Second, because, before taking action so final as an extraction, other solutions would be considered.

It all seems obvious yet, when it comes to business problems, outsiders seem all too willing and ready to provide an instant diagnosis and an instant cure; especially for the 'favoured' targets of disdain like British Rail or the Health Service. 'The trouble with X is . . . What they should do is . . . !'

If the problem was that easy to solve, there would be no problem! The first rule should therefore be obvious: no snap diagnosis, no instant cure. Instead, a thorough analysis of all the factors is needed before you draw any conclusions, and this implies that it is that *every* aspect of the organisation has to be analysed.

A useful word here is 'audit', but not in the traditional sense of an examination of the accounts of a company to establish that the money side of the affairs is reflected correctly in them; rather, an audit in the wider sense, signifying a thorough examination of all the parts of the organisation.

It is, however, appropriate to begin with the accounting and statistical information of the organisation because using numbers helps to pinpoint more accurately relative strengths and weaknesses. For example, to say 'the managers are a bunch of old men' is not as believable as 'the average age of the managers is 63.2 years'. Similarly to say 'our distribution costs are too high' is only credible if the statement can be proved in numbers, like '25p per mile compared to the average for the industry of 18.5p per mile'.

To be really helpful, numbers need to be handled in a special way. It is of very little use to say, 'Last year the factory produced 2½ million sausage rolls', because it is impossible to make any judgement about the number. It is better to compare the number with the previous year or with the competition: 'Last year we produced 2½ million sausage rolls, almost 400 thousand more than in the previous year and more than any of our competitors.' Moreover if the object of the exercise is to assess such things as efficiency and productivity, it is even better to use percentages and other ratios like cost per hour and output per man: 'Last year we produced 52 thousand sausage rolls per man compared with only 42 thousand per man in the previous year.'

It is only when the numbers are used in this way that the manager can begin to make valid assessments of the strength or weakness of the different areas of the organisation. The above example is looking at productivity in a sausage roll bakery and the conclusion that can be drawn from the data is that productivity has risen considerably – a sign of strength.

The important idea in all this is the need to compare and it is virtually impossible to draw any sensible conclusion about any bit of information unless it is compared.

Standards for making comparisons

Having established the need to make comparisons if we are going to make sensible statements about parts of organisations, the next question to answer is, What can we compare our information with? There can be four such standards for comparison. They are:

- the past
- other units in the same organisation
- other organisations
- internal targets or standards

The past

The main value in comparing what is going on now with what happened in earlier months or years is that it enables the analyst to identify trends. If he can then state whether the trend is favourable or unfavourable then he has identified strong or weak points in the organisation. For instance, if the management of a furniture works found that the quantity of waste wood was increasing (relative to the total amount used) then they would have a good indication of a weakness within the business.

Other units within the organisation

This kind of comparison is easily made in such organisations as Boots or Tesco, where statistics relating to measures of efficiency such as sales per square foot, sales per employee and profit per £100 of sales are compared from shop to shop. A manager of a particular store can identify what needs to be tackled to raise efficiency to the level of the best in the company.

Other organisations

At the beginning of this chapter, success was discussed and it was noted that organisations that are very successful have many strong points. However there is in every type of activity only one 'best'; all the others are less successful. This is why in sport there are league tables, why there is a hit parade for pop music, why there are 'pub of the year' and 'horse of the year' competitions. All are an attempt to find the best in that particular area of activity – the one which has minimised its weaknesses and has many strengths. For the rest of the competitors, if they want to improve they must seriously compare themselves against the best both to see how far behind they are and, more important, what it is that makes the best so successful. In soccer the question is, Why is the team at the top successful? Not just that it gets more points or has a better goal difference, but because of the way it goes about its job.

League tables in the world of business are not as common as in football, but they do exist in one form or another, and it is interesting keeping a lookout for them. Products themselves are analysed in such magazines as *Which?* but the information about companies is much less detailed. The magazine *Management Today* publishes league tables relating to the overall performance of the biggest companies in Britain (but using for the criterion the market value of the company. Thus it omits quite a number of well-known firms operating in Britain which happen not to have shares quoted on the Stock Exchange). There is also an annual publication called *The Times 1,000*, which contains basic information on all the biggest firms in Britain.

These are, however, fairly superficial league tables and do not provide much clue as to where the strengths and weaknesses of firms lie. To get at this kind of data it is usual to be a member of a trade association and also to contribute information to a kind of data bank about your own organisation. In addition to trade associations, one independent firm carries out this kind of activity, namely the Centre for Interfirm Comparison Ltd. This company not only compiles league tables of firms in specific sectors of business, but carries out a sophisticated analysis of each firm's data in fine detail, so that the relative strong and weak points of each can be clearly and positively identified. The main rule, so far as the Centre for Interfirm Comparison is concerned, is that you only get the league tables and the analysis if you yourself submit your organisation's data.

This kind of comparative analysis is not confined to manufacturing industry. Indeed the Centre for Interfirm Comparison carries out studies in sectors as diverse as libraries, hospitals, firms of solicitors and publishing houses as well. In addition, various local government activities (like education) benefit from this kind of approach.

Internal targets or standards

If performance is compared against a target set earlier then any failure to reach that target can be regarded as a weak point, assuming of course that the target was realistic and sensible in the first place. A good example of this is the target set for salesmen of taking orders each week of at least £10,000. So long as the target is reached, everyone is happy, but persistent failure by only one salesman signifies a problem. This type of comparison is limited to identifying current operational weaknesses and is more appropriate for keeping things under control, as we will see in Chapter 11.

What to look at to find strengths and weaknesses

It was suggested earlier that the whole organisation has to be analysed to make sure that all the significant areas of weakness and strength are identified. There are a number of ways of going about it, but one way is to look at the key areas of the organisation in turn. But first, the question that has to be asked is, Overall how is the organisation getting on? This implies that it must know what its primary objective is, so that it can measure how far off its actual performance was.

The objective will have been set with some regard to the best experience in the field, so ideally there is a three-way comparison:

actual *v.* objective
actual *v.* the best
objective *v.* the best

This gives a good indication of overall weakness and strength: the greater the gap between actual and the best or objectives then (assuming the best is higher) there are many specific areas of weakness to be identified.

Key areas to examine

1 *Financial resources*

Two issues are of major concern in this critical area of the business: the financial strength of the firm and the extent of risk.

Financial strength centres on how much money a company has and how much it can generate from its operations, or raise, or borrow and pay interest on its debts. Unfortunately, shortage of money seems to be a popular weakness these days, even in companies that are doing well by other criteria. A shortage of money may arise in a successful firm if considerable investment has just been made in new facilities, equipment or stocks, or if a takeover has just been completed involving cash. It is, in this case, only a weakness to be short of money in the sense that the firm does not have the freedom to do what it would like for a while.

A shortage of money is far more serious if it is coupled with an inability to borrow or raise money in any other way, especially if the amount of money tied up in easily convertible resources is low (for example in stocks or in money owed by customers, i.e. debtors). In this case the weakness can be fatal, causing the business to fold up.

Risk is the question of getting involved in activities which may fail (or may do extremely well). Risk is also affected by how much finance is tied up in foreign currencies which may be subject to adverse exchange rate changes. Financial risk itself usually refers to the extent to which a firm has borrowed money. This is often called 'Gearing' and is a serious weakness if the firm's trading performance is so poor that it cannot pay the interest on its debts, nor even pay back the money borrowed. On the other hand, the ability to borrow, or 'borrowing capacity', is a strength.

Financial strength makes most things possible; financial weakness makes only one thing possible if not cured – the close-down.

2 *Physical resources*

Companies need adequate physical facilities to keep costs down, provide for additional business and, where customers are concerned, give a quick and pleasant service.

Old buildings and equipment are not only unattractive but also often relatively inefficient. Reliability becomes a problem and maintenance expenditure goes up. Old equipment may also be technologically out of date (especially in the computer world).

As far as capacity of physical resource is concerned, it would seem at first thought that a firm operating at full capacity has a strength. It is, though, a weakness because it limits the capacity of the business to grow. Several successful football clubs have near-capacity attendances every time the first team plays at home. It is for them a real weakness that they cannot expand accommodation and so be even more successful. Similarly, companies may also find themselves short of space, particularly if they want to expand sales in an area of the country. If they have only limited warehouse space, then it is useless having a super-efficient sales force because the sales could not get to the customer. The thoughtful manager will identify the weakness first and cure it before attempting to expand.

Another example of capacity being a weakness is where a firm's equipment is working flat-out. Clearly there is little point in having a huge advertising campaign designed to increase sales substantially if no more output could be obtained. First the weakness (i.e. not enough equipment) has to be cured.

A further physical resource element to be considered is the actual location of the firm. It is clearly a weakness for a company based in Cornwall if its major market or major supplier is in Glasgow. To be near the source of materials, or markets is a major strength.

3 Human resources

The human resource is every firm's most important resource and two main elements need to be studied: Age and Skills.

AGE factors. We have seen that old physical resources can be regarded as a weakness, and the same applies to the human resource. To have a very high proportion of old people is a weakness, not because they are old as such, but because, if they all retire at once, so much knowledge and experience will disappear overnight that the company is left much weaker. Ideally, companies employ people of all ages in equal proportions at any one time or, some prefer a few young and a few old with most in the middle. Would you fancy the British Lions' rugby XV's chances if the average age of the team was sixteen? Would you fancy its chances any more if the average age was thirty-nine? At work, would you enjoy working in an office where all the others were either under twenty or over sixty?

SKILLS factors. Even the most successful companies usually find that they do not possess people with first-class skills in all areas of the operation. The easiest example to cite is a football club: all would like to have eleven players with super skills, but nearly all of them have to put up with some good, some indifferent and some worse. Likewise, all managers would like to have a first-class team working for them, but the dream is hard to turn into reality. However, identifying the weak points is part of the manager's job and he has to cure them, either by training or by replacement.

Personnel audit

A personnel audit should reveal the age composition of the staff and a profile of their skills. Many companies have failed to make new ventures succeed because they did not recognise that their staff did not have sufficient skills in the new areas.

Products and services

A well-developed range of products or services is one of a company's greatest strengths. Conversely a firm with weak products seems to struggle to keep afloat. Among the key factors to examine are: price levels (higher or lower than the competition), share of the market and loss of appeal. This latter aspect is particularly important: sooner or later every product or service ever invented loses its appeal and people stop buying it. There are many reasons for this: tastes change, new designs emerge, competition produces a better or cheaper alternative but some seem to go on for ever (like a packet of tea). This whole idea is embodied in the notion of the 'product life-cycle', an important concept in assessing strengths and weaknesses. Many successful firms achieve their position because their products are at their peak. Unfortunately, today's popular product will be tomorrow's lame duck, so regard has to be paid to where products are in the cycle. Ideally they would all be at different stages of life, some just starting, some growing, some at maturity and some declining.

Buying

The buying problem has already been mentioned (page 29). In many organisations, strength in the buying area is critical if the business is to survive. The big retail grocery chains operate on such tiny profit margins that a two per cent increase in the price of purchases can halve profits. In nearly all firms that handle products (except the most labour intensive) the cost of purchases by far outweighs the cost of labour, hence the importance of strong buying.

Selling and promotion

It is important to make sure that selling and promotion are strong if growth of sales is envisaged. Questions such as the extent to which the sales force covers the territory and how well it penetrates the outlets for the products of the company have to be answered. So has the extent to which promoting the organisation's goods or services is carried out, compared to the competition.

Research and development

An area that must not be forgotten, because strength in this facility can be the key to a prosperous future. A weak research and development team helps nobody.

Management

As well as an audit of all employees, special regard has to be given to an audit of management. Because it is not just the age profile of these people, nor their technical and professional skills that are important, it is the ability to manage that determines whether the future will be bright or not. Issues such as leadership skill, business appreciation, vision and decision-making ability are all essential ingredients in the strong management profile.

The organisation

In looking at the individual trees it is easy to lose sight of the shape of the forest, and in terms of organisations the whole must be studied as well as its component parts. In particular there are four aspects to which attention should be paid.

- *Structure* – the actual organisational set-up as set out in an organisation chart. Who reports to whom? Who is responsible for what?
- *Systems* – the methods used to make sure things get done (or to prevent things going wrong).
- *Policies* – the rules which govern many of the decisions of the organisation (how to sell; where to buy; where to sell; who not to employ etc.).

If these three are operating properly nobody is aware of them, but if they are wrong they can strangle the life out of an organisation. This will be discussed later, in Chapters 6 and 11.

The fourth and last part of the overall organisation question is

■ *Atmosphere and morale*

Have you ever been into an office, a club or a meeting and been aware of a depressing atmosphere? Conversely, you may have been somewhere (or even worked in a place) which seemed to hum with a sense of purpose. Pubs and restaurants carry atmospheres strongly and so do football clubs near the end of season, especially where promotion or relegation is concerned.

To try to build up an organisation if there is poor morale or atmosphere is pointless. You have to rebuild morale first.

Some of the key audit questions discussed are set out below in the form of a checklist. You may like to use it to assess the overall strength and weakness rating of the organisation you work for or know best, or indeed for your own department.

If any of the questions are irrelevant substitute for them areas important in your own context. Remember that the list is not comprehensive and there may be more factors of importance.

You may not be able to get hold of suitable comparative information, so you have to use your own judgement to decide whether a particular factor suggests strength or weakness.

Twenty key corporate audit questions

Area of the business	Question
Buying	■ Are we buying cheapest and best without too high stock levels?

Physical	■ Are our physical resources modern and efficient? ■ Do we have adequate extra space for, and capacity in, both production and stores? ■ Are we located in the right places?
Products	■ Where are they in the product life-cycle? ■ What shares of their market do they have? ■ Are prices too high, too low or about right?
Sales and promotion	■ Do the sales force sell to enough customers? ■ Do we advertise and promote as much as the competition?
Research and Development	■ Are we putting enough effort into it?
People	■ How good is the age and skills structure of our employees?
Managers	■ Included in the last question; and are they giving good leadership?
Finance	■ How much extra money could we raise either by borrowing or in share capital? ■ Are we at risk financially (eg because of foreign exchange fluctuations or because of high interest payments)?
Organisation	■ Is the structure appropriate? ■ Are the systems a millstone? ■ Are the firm's policies sensible? ■ How good is the atmosphere and morale?

Overall   ■ How profitable are we?

Finally, the extent to which an internal appraisal is carried out depends on the size and complexity of the company and also on the degree of success it is enjoying. It is easy to ignore the exercise when things are going well – only to wake up and discover you are in difficulties. The wise manager is continuously evaluating performance to nip malaise in the bud and to push home the advantages that stem from strength.

How to cure weaknesses? Sometimes it is obvious, sometimes it requires considerable expertise. Some indications are given later in this book, but for particular complex problems it would be wiser to turn to books or experts on the area of concern itself.

4 Planning: The Business Environment

All companies are affected by events outside their control, and a firm's survival and success depends on how skillfully its managers handle these external influences. A company that does no planning is trusting that the future will stay much the same as today. In contrast, the firm that tries to anticipate how its environment is changing stands a much better chance of prospering. Consider the case of the Vanishing Paper Shop:

> This particular shop was situated on a busy main road midway between the town centre and the railway station (and an easy walk to either). It picked up a lot of passing trade, as well as people walking to and from the station. In addition, nearby was a popular sports ground and a lot of business was done on match days. The business was very prosperous and was always well stocked with a wide range of goods.
>
> Then one day something happened. The owner was the same, the products were the same, the assistants were the same and the owner had done nothing different. Yet business simply disappeared, and within a few weeks the shop closed and the owner opened up another shop elsewhere in a much less suitable location.

What happened that caused the business to fall so dramatically? Simply that double yellow lines were painted along both sides of the road passing the shop and there was nowhere to park. So, motorists no longer stopped there and the locals found it inconvenient: you could no longer jump in the car and pop round for a birthday card or some ice-cream. The business depended on that kind of trade for its prosperity and, without it, Vanishing Paper Shop became just another 'average' shop.

Events occurred outside the owner's control. There was little he could do about the double yellow lines in the road. This kind of unplanned, unforeseen, unexpected event has been recognised for many years and has become popularly known as Sod's Law or Murphy's Law; no matter how carefully things are planned the most unlikely event will occur to thwart you. The things outside one's control are the events that take place in the outside world or, to give it the smart name, the 'environment'. There would be no problem if the environment was stable and never changed; unfortunately it does change and (just to make things even more interesting) the rate of change is not consistent.

To illustrate this idea, look outside at the weather. Most of us live in places where the weather is changeable, and the weather you are experiencing now will not go on for ever. You know it is going to change but what you do not know is:

- *when* it is going to change; and
- *what* it is going to change to.

It is probably easier to look at the problem in a different way by asking the questions, For how long is the present weather likely to continue? And, When it changes is it likely to change for the better or the worse?

Climate is, of course, one of the most unpredictable environments, although fortunately the range of possible types of weather that any one place at any one time can experience is fairly limited. Moreover there is an annual cycle which can fairly safely be predicted a long time ahead even though actual daily conditions may not be accurately forecast – for example that on 2 January 2000 the weather in Liverpool will be fairly cold.

Future events are, therefore, of two kinds; the predictable (the weather is unlikely to be very hot; the National Westminster Bank is unlikely to go broke) and the unpredictable (the precise temperature in Liverpool; the precise profits of the National Westminster Bank in 2000).

Climate is just one environmental factor in hundreds that affect organisations to a greater or lesser extent, and many of these factors are highly unpredictable. Consider Liverpool on 2 January 2000. What will be the demand for home computers on that day? How many gallons of petrol will be wanted? How many bottles of tomato sauce will be sold? There is no way of answering these questions with any degree of precision. Indeed, in some cases the product or service may have disappeared completely (imagine a world without tomato sauce). It may be argued that there is no need to worry about what things will be like so far into the future – the 'let's cross that bridge when we come to it' argument. That kind of argument has a great deal of appeal; unfortunately it can lead to disaster. For instance, suppose your firm is a major supplier of petrol to garages in Liverpool and you believe that, in 2000, the total number of gallons of petrol needed will be twenty times what it is now. What do you do? You set about making sure that the facilities are available to cope with the demand for petrol. More garages would be needed, more lorries to transport the fuel and, or course, to be sure of having the petrol itself it may be necessary to start exploring for oil now. Failure to respond now will ruin the chances of trading successfully in the future.

A small shop may be able to adapt fairly quickly to most changes, although even in that case, as we saw at the beginning of the chapter, there is always an exception. It would appear that as organisations grow and get more complicated so it takes longer and longer to change their set-up to meet changes in the environment. A small boat can change direction quickly, but it takes a giant supertanker a lot of miles and quite a time to change its course. Many new developments can take over ten years from start to full operation – aircraft and nuclear power stations are good examples – simply because they are so complicated and expensive to design, develop and build.

The questions which need to be considered regarding the environment, and to which we now turn, are:

- What aspects of the environment have to be taken into account in planning and what can safely be ignored?
- Is there any way of anticipating what is going to happen?
- How far ahead should organisations try to estimate what is going to happen?
- How can an organisation minimise the threats from the environment that lie ahead and take advantage of the opportunities that may exist?

What aspects of the environment (outside world) have to be taken into account?

A case for thinking about

A large company owned a nice hotel in the middle of a pleasant prosperous town. During the week the forty bedrooms were usually fully occupied, mainly by businessmen, and the restaurant and bars were always busy. At weekends in summer the hotel was popular with tourists breaking their journeys.

A proposal was made to increase the number of

bedrooms by twenty, each with bath, shower and toilet. It was calculated that, to make a reasonable return on the cost of the project, all the extra rooms would have to be occupied at least every other night on average. This meant that because of the slack winter weekend trade, during the week an extra twenty guests would have to turn up each night.

The question was, if they built the bedrooms could they be sure of getting the extra business? Inquiries showed that people liked the hotel, the prices were reasonable and the only competition was a similar sized hotel on the outskirts of town.

The question was put by the managing director like this: 'If we start now we could open the new bedrooms in three years' time. Will the demand for bedrooms be so much higher then that all twenty rooms will be filled on three nights a week and just a few let the rest of the time?' There was no good answer to that question because nobody had the ability to see into the future, but the manager of the hotel said: 'Demand has been growing over the last few years and I can see no good reason for it to stop.' To this the chief accountant, who tended to get a bit unhappy if people wanted to spend money, responded: 'Well, I can think of at least half a dozen reasons why demand could stop growing . . .'

Among the reasons that the accountant gave for his belief that the demand for rooms in their hotel would not grow were:

- The next government would be the present opposition and they would clamp down on expense accounts for businessmen.
- The next government would also not spend so much money helping industry (by not giving research grants, etc.).
- The rising cost of fuel was going to put more and more people on to trains, planes and buses or

coaches. There would be much more attempt to get 'there and back in a day', especially as trains were getting faster.

- There was likely to be an economic recession soon and organisations would be less likely to give their staff a free hand about travelling around. There would be less money to spend generally.
- The increase in demand had been associated with a growth in the number of organisations based in the town. That growth 'might well come to an end'.
- The competitor would not stand idly by to let us cream off the demand. They would build too, and *they* had space for a swimming pool.
- Social pressure was building up (as in Sweden) against businessmen spending even a couple of nights away from home. Increasingly people would be expected not to be away overnight.

All these reasons reflect aspects of the hotel's environment which could affect it and it is possible to group the possibilities into several different types of environment. This helps to make analysis more effective.

The first two answers relate to government and could be called the 'political and legal' environment. The second example was also dealing with money matters and this, along with the third, could be described as the 'economic' environment. The third is also dealing with a technological issue and so we could refer to a 'technological' environment. Fourth and fifth are also economic (but at different levels). Sixth is the 'competitive' environment, and the last example is suggesting a social trend and is a 'social' environment.

These six different environments (including natural phenomena like the weather) are a convenient way of classifying the world around the organisation, and each one needs a closer look.

The political and legal environment

All organisations have to exist within the political and legal system wherever they operate. At home, politics can be national or local and both can have a significant effect on the life and well-being of the organisation. If the political party in power never changed, or if its policies never changed, then life would be very simple. But it is the way of political life, in Britain at any rate, that it changes frequently; sometimes organisations feel themselves blown to and fro as the political power base changes to the extent that they do not know what attitudes to adopt themselves.

Some political parties are prepared to spend money, others are not. Some will have free trade policies and encourage organisations to set up in different countries and export and import their goods and services. Others do not welcome that kind of activity. As far as an organisation is concerned that operates across national frontiers, the worst type of country to deal with is the one with political instability, because you never know if the next group to come to power will favour you.

It is not only in relation to trade and business that the political environment is important, but in many other respects. Some governments seem to delight in creating laws that increase the number of forms that have to be filled in. Others, both at a local and national level, have an attitude of letting organisations get on with it and do not interfere. On the other hand there are those which pass many laws of a restrictive nature effectively making it illegal for organisations to do certain things.

All organisations have to live within an active political environment and have to be aware that what they do could be the object of some political action.

The economic environment

Probably no organisation can avoid being affected by the economic environment. Again the state of the economy is continuously changing and the organisation that succeeds is the one that identifies rising and falling trends fastest and takes action soonest, or which has sufficient flexibility to adapt to a new economic situation. The fastest responses to changing economic environments are seen on Budget Day when the Chancellor of the Exchequer announces an increase in the tax on petrol and alcoholic drink. Instantly queues form up at petrol stations and all the off-licences do a roaring trade. Some individuals are a bit slow off the mark and arrive just as stocks run out, but others – the ones who have taken a chance – made their purchases a day or two before because they felt the probability of increased duty was very high.

The economic environment has many aspects and the main ones that affect organisations are:

The prosperity of the market. Using the word 'market' in its widest possible sense to mean all the possible customers for the organisation's goods or services, it is not hard to see that if customers are not feeling well off they are not likely to spend much. For example, the amount of business a public house does reflects fairly well how prosperous the market is. The story is virtually the same for all organisations that sell products or services, but some are much more sensitive to the ups and downs of the economy than others. Firms in the motor trade are very vulnerable, because the sale of new cars falls off rapidly when times are not so good; the problem for motor dealers especially is that they buy from the manufacturer in anticipation of being able to sell the cars. If, however, the customers do not come into the showrooms and buy, the dealer is left with a heap of new cars, little money in the bank and the problem of paying next week's wages.

Inflation. Inflation is known to everyone as increases in the price we have to pay for goods in the shops. All organisations, in inflationary times, find that they have to pay out more for the goods and services they are using than they were before. Raw materials' costs rise, wages rise, electricity and petrol prices increase and so on. For a time organisations can overcome this by increasing the prices of their own goods and services to compensate. But people have a habit of resisting and there comes a point when the price increase causes a big drop in demand. Some organisations try to beat inflation by anticipating increases in commodities and buy before the price goes up. The hard part is guessing which products are going to go up in price and when.

Exchange rates. Organisations that are involved in buying from other countries or which sell into other countries, as well as those that are set up in more than one state, are particularly concerned about the way exchange rates fluctuate, because a great deal of money can be lost if the wrong currency is being held at the wrong time. Moreover, buying goods from overseas at the wrong time can cost a great deal of profit, just as selling into an overseas market at the wrong time can also bring in less income.

Interest rates. Interest is the cost of borrowing as well as the reward of lending, and these days there are very few organisations that manage without at some time having to borrow money. There are many advantages in borrowing (and there are risks too), but the timing of that borrowing can be critical. For instance, a company wanted to borrow £½ million to equip a new factory with modern machinery. They were offered the money at 10 per cent interest, but they failed to take action fast enough and by the time they got round to it the cheapest offer they could get was 11½ per cent interest. The delay cost the firm £7,500 a year in extra interest.

The technological environment

Is there much demand these days for gas lights, slide-rules or mangles? It is fairly plain that gas is no longer used for lighting, calculators have replaced slide-rules and the washing machine's spin-dry facility has finished off the mangle. All these are simple examples of products that are no longer any use because something better has come along to do the job (or in some cases make the job obsolete).

The changes in the technological environment (using technology here in a very wide sense) that have been seen over the last thirty years are immense, particularly in such areas as chemicals, drugs and electronics. Space-age technology is the advertising man's way of describing many of the products in our homes or for sale in the shops – from cameras to ceramic cooker tops. Whether the speed of technological change is accelerating or not does not really matter (some people say it is, some say it is not). What is important is that there is a lot of change about and organisations have to be aware of the possibilities in three ways.

First, there is the problem that competitors may achieve a technological development which may bite into your own market. What is worse is an entirely new form of opposition from a different type of competitor. For instance, the electrically driven motorcar is being developed by the existing car makers, and also by a battery maker.

Second, organisations have to be aware of general

technological advances in the broad area which they can build into their own products.

Third, all organisations use equipment of one kind or another, even if it is only the normal range of office equipment – typewriter, photocopier, telephones. Technology is updating all the equipment used by organisations at a very fast rate. The managing director of the British side of a multinational organisation manufacturing heavy equipment said that the hardest part of his job was nothing to do with unions, pay or products, but whether to spend money on the latest technologically improved equipment (like the latest telephone switchboard or automatic typing machines or even 'robotics' – the silicon-chip-based machines that copy human movement).

The point is that the organisation that fails to keep up to date will die (how many dentists still use a foot-powered drill?), but the organisation that kicks off the development of a new piece of technology very often succeeds. Xerox photocopiers and Polaroid cameras are both examples of being first and staying winners.

Competition

Possibly the best-known element in the environment for most firms is competition. 'Know your enemy' is an old military saying and it applies to business just as much, because firms that are in competition with each other are trying to do each other down. Even within organisations there may be rivalries, by no means an uncommon occurrence. The first problem for a company is often to define exactly who the competition is. For instance, in recent years there has been an advertising campaign for tea using the slogan 'best drink of the day'.

A few moments' thought about what competes with

tea reveals just how wide competition can actually be.

Coffee is the obvious competitor, being called a beverage like tea; but tea is, more broadly, a drink, and once we start listing the different types of drink it seems that the whole world is lined up to compete with tea – even water is a competitor.

It is the job of the marketing man to study the market in which the product competes to establish not just what are the competitors but, more important, which are the relevant competitors. A relevant competitor is a product which could be a replacement for your product – or which could lose out to your product. If tea is seen as something to wake you up in the morning then its obvious competitors are coffee, milk and fruit juice. Gin and brandy are not relevant competitors in that context (at least not to most people). Each of the products tries to take away customers from the other, and if one product fails to secure for itself an identifiable niche with a steady body of support then sooner or later it gets too weak to exist.

This situation applies to commercial organisations of every kind, not just those making products. Shops, hotels, road transport firms, advertising agencies and so on all have to recognise and deal with competition.

Companies, therefore, spend a good deal of time and effort finding out about the competition, through market research, market intelligence and business analysis. It is not difficult to find out something about one's competitors and their products; the hard part is finding out about those firms who are going to compete against you *next year* – the firm that is not in your market, but is looking at it as a possible new venture. Various Japanese companies have entered into world markets over the last twenty-five to thirty years quite unexpectedly in many cases: motorcycles, watches and motorcars being the best-known examples. Recently the lawnmower industry has demonstrated that it is possible to anticipate such an event and has taken early steps to combat the entrance of a new competitor.

Social

The social environment of an organisation can change as much as any of the other types of environment. Often the changes are not so dramatic as a new technology, for instance, and this makes them less easy to identify until their impact cannot be avoided. An obvious social change is the way in which the number going to the cinema declined, slowly and steadily, year after year.

Another example is the way in which smoking has become less sociably acceptable and is continuing to be less and less popular. In fact there are strong social pressures against tobacco products, and these have led to specific political moves such as the abolition of cigarette advertising on television. Very often this tide of opinion, of changing social values, is impossible to reverse once it has gained some standing. If an organisation fails to recognise the trend – or tries to fight back – sooner or later it will lose out. The tobacco companies have recognised the trend in society's attitude to smoking and have adopted, deliberately, programmes for investing in other, more acceptable, products.

Natural

One of the most important parts of the natural environment is the weather, as we have already seen. It is obviously relevant in farming, building and cricket, and of importance to the makers of such products as ice cream and soft drinks. These companies find that as the temperature rises sales increase and as the temperature falls sales decline. Have you ever heard the expression 'we didn't do as well as we'd hoped because of the bad winter (or spring, or summer?)'? It is the most plausible and understandable excuse in the world for poor performance. Yet in reality it is simply saying 'we failed to consider the possibility that the weather may be no good for us'. It is quite astonishing how many people and organisations are surprised and unprepared when it snows in January.

Another key climatic factor is that relating to crop yields; the famous example of Brazilian coffee is a case in point. In Brazil, frost strikes occasionally, and if it is severe enough the coffee crop can be reduced substantially. A company in Europe using coffee can be in difficulties if it fails to get its supplies on time at the right prices; these firms have to be on their guard against the possibility of such an event.

Another important natural aspect of the environment is population and its structure – not in general but in the areas where the firm trades and is located. If the population where you sell is shrinking, alternatives have to be found to maintain sales revenue levels. If the population is getting older and there are fewer children, you have a problem if you sell prams and baby-clothes.

Another important natural aspect of the environment is population and its structure – not in general but in the area where the organisation operates. Put simply, if you think there are going to be more youngsters you build schools. If you think there are going to be more old people you build hospitals.

Is there any way of anticipating what is going to happen?

On page 63 four questions were posed and the subsequent discussion has been on finding a way of classifying the environment to help us minimise the threats that the future may bring and to help us grab the opportunities that may present themselves.

To the next question – can we anticipate what might happen? – the short answer is 'no, not precisely'; if the future were easy to predict there would be no gambling. Nevertheless there has to be an attempt, and several specific aids are available to try to reduce the lack of uncertainty about the future.

'Futurology' is the name given to the business of trying to assess what the environment might look like in a number of years ahead. One of the most famous futurologists is an American called Herman Kahn whose detailed pictures of the world in the future make fascinating reading.* What Kahn and others do is paint a picture of the world as it might appear a number of years ahead. Anyone can produce these 'scenarios' as they are called, by identifying current trends and extending the idea into the future as far as you want.

The Delphi technique

This is named after the ancient oracle at Delphi in Greece, which was famous from the eighth to the fifth century BC for the forecasts it made. Nowadays the forecasts are made by consulting experts in the subject under review rather than by the priestess of Apollo. In outline, the technique is to see if a number of experts in a subject agree on some future event. If thirty experts

* *The Year 2000: A framework for speculation on the next thirty-three years* is the title of one of his books (Macmillan, 1967), written with A. J. Wiener.

in vehicle engineering agree that the electric motorcar will be commonplace by 1995, you may decide to sell your petrol station on the basis of their opinion. They could, of course, be totally wrong, but this is unlikely.

Economic models

A popular way of looking ahead in the economic world is to set up an imaginary economy on a computer and feed it with a lot of information. Hopefully the results that come out will give an indication of the state of the economy from one year to five or six years ahead. (Some people have gone up to 2100 AD but not really seriously.) The only problem is that there has to be an assumption that people, organisations and governments will behave in certain ways. So often the conclusions are qualified with statements like 'assuming no change in government policy'. Even so they are useful indicators, especially in the short term, of the way the economy is going.

How far ahead should organisations try to estimate what is going to happen?

The answer depends on the problem. If you want to do an hour's gardening now you do not need tomorrow's weather forecast. What you do want is some way of being able to have enough time to plan your own response to some future event. To use an example from defence strategy, if it takes your airforce three minutes to get to a combat level, there is little point in having a radar system that tells you when a missile is two minutes from your territory. You need more time and this is only obtainable if you can pick up signals on your radar at least four minutes' equivalent distance away. One writer in this area, Igor Ansoff, talks about picking up weak signals from the environment.* In other words the organisation has got to try to look far enough into the future so that it has time to prepare (if it picks up that weak signal). One successful British company habitually makes economic forecasts two years ahead. It saw the recession of 1980 early in 1979 and made its plans accordingly (cutting its capital expenditure plans). On the other hand one organisation only realised the problem in the autumn of 1980 and found that it had to continue with its projects because it would have been more expensive to stop. It had, therefore, to cut expenditure in other, more sensitive, areas – including considerable staff redundancies.

The distance to look into the future is called the 'planning horizon' – a time in the future that the organisation can 'see' with a reasonable degree of confidence. At one extreme most small shops will have a planning horizon for most things of a few days (a greengrocer has a 24-hour horizon). The larger and more sophisticated the firm the longer the horizon.

Some organisations do not need to worry about long-term effects because their environment is relatively stable or their activities are not especially sensitive to most happenings. Shoe shops are a good example of organisations that come into this category. There are, in contrast, some whose activities are very sensitive to the changes in the environment, which may itself be very unstable. An excellent example of that is the 'rag trade', the business of garment manufacture, especially ladies' fashions. It is subject to many environmental changes, some of which are very volatile and sudden, yet it has to plan new designs well ahead of the season; this year's autumn collection was being planned at least eighteen months ago in successful firms and nego-

* H. Igor Ansoff, *Strategic Management* (Macmillan, 1979).

tiations were taking place with the buyers from the shops.

How can a company minimise the threats and take advantage of the opportunities?

The fourth question posed on page 63 recognises that every firm's environment changes: sometimes the change is favourable and the wind blows the right way; other times the storm clouds gather and steps have to be taken to make sure the company is not blown off course. The 'course' itself is, in management terms, the 'strategy', for which see the next chapter. Changes in the environment that can be seen a long way off can be built into the strategy, but sudden change demands two important managerial skills – first the ability to recognise the change (too often managers behave like ostriches and pretend the problem either does not exist or that it will quietly go away). Second, managers must be decisive enough to change things within the firm when the going looks rough, by abandoning old ways and adopting new ones.

Finally it is a mistake to think that all this analysis is carried out by top management only. All managers have a responsibility to be aware of the factors that affect the firm, both generally and as they affect their own spheres of responsibility . . . it is their jobs that are at risk in the end, as well as the health of the firm.

5 Planning: Strategic Decisions

It is not specially difficult to set objectives in business; the hard part is in deciding how to achieve those objectives. This is the realm of strategic management, a technique that has become very important in business over the last twenty years.

What is strategy?

Consider an example of strategy formulation from outside the business world – the world of mountain climbing, a popular activity in summer. One of the favourite mountains is Snowdon in North Wales, which on a sunny day in August is crowded with walkers and climbers. Part of its attraction is the fact that it is the highest mountain in England and Wales, but in addition it has spectacular views from the summit (if you are lucky) and there is a restaurant just below the summit to quench the thirst.

The interesting thing about Snowdon is that there are no less than nine or ten recognised, normal routes up to the summit, seven different starting points and countless uncommon routes frequented only by rock climbers. Some of the ways up are easy – there is a railway to within a few yards of the top – some are long and laborious. Others are short but need special rock-climbing equipment and skills – otherwise they are virtually impossible and exceedingly dangerous.

If you choose to climb Snowdon, the most important decision to make is the route itself, and we can refer to this decision as the 'strategic decision'. Of course, the word 'strategy' is not normally used in relation to a mountain in Britain, but it certainly is used in describing the broad way of tackling peaks in the Himalayas or Andes. This is neatly illustrated in the book *Everest the Hard Way* by Chris Bonington.* In the foreword Lord Hunt, who led the successful Everest expedition of 1952, writes 'Upon no one was the stress so great and so prolonged as on the leader of the expedition. His was the original decision to make the bid; his the choice of companions, the general strategy, the supervision of the whole complex plan and its unfolding on Everest'.

Later in the book Bonington refers to himself as a 'frustrated field-marshal' which is apt because strategy actually refers to 'leading an army'. Today the word is used extensively and has become quite common in management literature, although its use is not restricted to leading people. Strategy is not concerned with details; rather it is concerned with basic directions, broad intentions and the general approach to the problem. Our decision to climb Snowdon comes first; then we decide the general strategy which may be expressed like this. 'We will ascend by the route known as the Watkin Path and return the same way, leaving the car in the car park at the bottom. We will climb it on the first fine day we get next week.'

It is easy to see what strategy means if we are referring to a journey, an expedition or a war. It is not so obvious how it relates to the problem of companies reaching their objectives. A good example of a business strategic problem is in the case of a high street shoe shop, which one day discovered that the rent had been doubled. The manager decided that something of significance had to be done to restore the shop to its former level of profitability and he knew that the natural rate

* Hodder and Stoughton, 1976.

of growth of the market would be insufficient. There were plenty of ideas, including painting the shop-front to make it more attractive, extending the opening hours by half an hour each day, get the lady assistants to sell men's shoes, advertise, and sell socks and stockings. The only action which could be described as strategic is the last one, because that is the only one concerned with a major shift in the emphasis of the business. The others, to a greater or lesser extent, are merely tinkering with the existing system. The problem was to get more money into the tills, and painting the place, opening longer and getting ladies to sell men's shoes would not solve the problem. A big change was needed, even bigger than an advertising campaign could produce in the circumstances (although advertising might have formed the marketing strategy to support the general strategy).

Steps in choosing strategies

Step 1: Where are we?

It may seem obvious, but you would not choose to climb Snowdon tomorrow if today you are in Paris. You would probably not choose to climb it tomorrow if you climbed it yesterday. Similarly a company would not try to double its sales of a particular product if it already held eighty-five per cent of the market. Unless it knows where it stands, however, it could waste a lot of time and energy pursuing the impossible.

Step 2: Where do we want to be?

Again it seems obvious, and as far as organisations are concerned all that needs adding is the answer to the question, When do we want to get there?

In terms of corporate objectives these two steps can be described like this: 'Our primary objective is a return on capital of twenty-five per cent in five years' time. Currently our actual return is only twelve per cent – the difference to be made up by selecting some suitable strategy.'

It is simple enough to draw this idea on a graph:

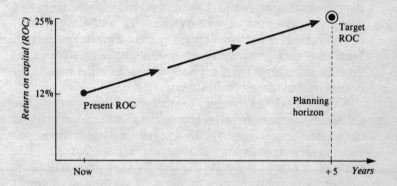

The line connecting the current return on capital with the target figure in five years' time is important only because the steepness of the slope indicates the size of the problem to be tackled. If your company is highly profitable now then the target may not be much higher

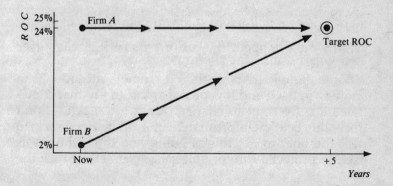

– so the line is almost horizontal. But if the firm has only a one or two per cent return and wants to be at twenty-five per cent, its line is so steep it looks 'unclimbable'.

It is not difficult to guess which of the two firms illustrated above has the best chance of reaching its five-year target ROC.

There is not much doubt that firm *A*, already earning twenty-four per cent, has a much better chance of achieving a return of twenty-five per cent than firm *B* down near the bottom which is only barely profitable. Firm *B* is not generating as much profit as needed to finance the climb up the chart, whereas all *A* has to do is use its resources to hang on.

These two examples represent firms near the extremes of the results typically found. Many firms obviously enjoy returns in excess of twenty-five per cent and many fail to make any money at all. The danger for the firm at the bottom of the league is obvious: its weak points make it so vulnerable it could easily fade away. Its strength is probably fear of extinction, which can do wonders for the ailing organisation.

On the other hand the danger for the organisation currently high in the league is *complacency* – letting things go on and assuming they will be OK. To identify this danger properly is the next step.

Step 3: Where will we be if we do nothing different?

What would happen to a car or a plane if it was never serviced?

Some people regard the 'do nowt' attitude as a strategy in itself and it is probably fair to say that sometimes it is best not to change things too much – don't 'rock the boat'. Unfortunately it's often necessary to rock the boat to get things going; too often the cry is used to protect a comfortable *status quo*. 'Don't rock the boat' can only be justified as a strategy if it is absolutely certain that you will reach your objective travelling the way you are.

It is, however, impossible to be certain that one's objective will be reached, especially in the long term. On the other hand it is a fairly safe bet that if no changes are made to the way the organisation carries out its tasks, sooner or later it will lose its prominent position and become another lame duck. There are thousands of examples of organisations that failed to move with the times, that tried to avoid having to make changes, that refused to adapt and innovate. The French Revolution is one of the most devastating examples of what happens if the 'do nowt' strategy is pursued to the bitter end. At the other end of the scale there is the corner shop that closed down because it never had a coat of paint, a new look or a new range of products.

Again the idea can be put on to our simple chart:

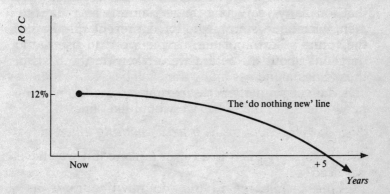

There are in fact many dozens of reasons why a 'no change' strategy could lead to failure, but in a nutshell either its internal operations have become inefficient, or some environmental threat has become a reality. In other words if you do nothing different your strengths evaporate, your weaknesses grow, the threats materialise and you cannot seize (or even see) any opportunities.

As far as strategy is concerned the 'do nothing new' line has to be calculated using information from the internal appraisal and the environment evaluation. This kind of projection into the future is normally called a 'forecast' – a simple statement of what will happen if present trends continue – and it is a very common activity especially in marketing.

There is little point in spending a lot of money advertising a product if it is going to sell like hot cakes anyway. Nor is there much point in redesigning the packaging of another product if it is clearly at the end of its life cycle.

Forecasts, then, assume that the organisation does nothing to meet the threats and opportunities coming up in the environment, and these reveal the downward slope sooner or later. Perhaps it should be noted here that for many years long-range planning as a management technique simply projected present trends into the future – 'extrapolation' is the word to use – and decisions about the future were taken on the basis of these lines alone.

It is a simple matter to superimpose the 'do nothing new' line on to the 'what we would like' line:

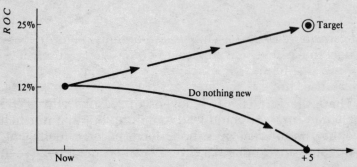

Three things have to be noted about this chart. First, each organisation's chart is different, depending on where it is at the present time and how fast its decline is projected.

Second, the two lines are together at first and may continue to be close for several years ahead. It would be a lucky organisation to be able to say with confidence that within five years nothing will happen to blow the firm off course.

The third point is that the gap between the two lines is gradually getting wider, and the size of the gap is of vital interest to the planner because it shows the size of the problem. It is known, quite simply, as the 'planning gap' – the difference between what will happen and what you would like to happen: forecast v. target.

Having identified the size of the planning gap the problem is the difficult one of choosing suitable strategies that will fill the gap. Before that can be done it is worth making a list of the main constraints that exist to prevent you doing what you want.

Step 4: What can we not do?

A detailed, complete list of things a company cannot do would be endless. Instead a 'top twenty' list of constraints can be constructed, some of which are the result of internal decisions and others which are imposed on the organisation from outside.

Internally generated constraints. All organisations deliberately make laws that stop them doing the most sensible thing in terms of efficiency or effectiveness. For instance, there is the manager of the pub who refuses to sell tobacco (or permit smoking inside). There is the company which logically should be situated in Central London but is located in Devon because the managing director runs a small orchard down there 'on the side'.

Another example is the business that refuses to buy materials and components from a particular supplier or country, and which refuses to sell its products to particular customers or countries.

There can be many reasons for these kinds of internal laws – religion, ethics, politics, personal preference or just plain bigotry being among the most common. They are important and must be kept separately from weaknesses, because weaknesses have to be dealt with, but constraints have to be lived with.

External constraints. The most obvious external constraints on organisations are those that come out of the laws of the land where the organisation is based. Of particular interest and importance are those laws and regulations which constrain the organisation in its day-to-day operations. Such things as hours of opening for shops, building regulations, rules about the use of certain chemicals including artificial flavourings and colourings in food products, and import and export regulations all limit the organisation's choice of ways of making progress (while hopefully protecting the public from the unscrupulous).

The difference between external threats and external constraints should be noted; a threat is something in the future but a constraint is something here and now imposed on the organisation.

Step 5: How do we fill the gap?

On the face of it there is not much difference between this question and the question that all business organisations have always asked, namely, How do we make more money? However, referring to the 'planning gap' is much less vague and it is a question that can be applied to any organisation since it is not limited to money.

The search for a suitable strategy can be undertaken in a number of ways; every management text book that discusses strategic planning seems to have its own system. In general, however, strategies can be grouped into three. They are:

- improve
- expand
- diversify

Each has distinct advantages and disadvantages.

Improvement strategies. Simply to have a strategy which concentrates on improving the efficiency or the effectiveness of the organisation seems to be rather dull and uninspiring. Improving means being better at doing existing things, and as we saw earlier there is no such thing as being 100 per cent efficient; there is always scope for being better. Of course it is not as easy to be more efficient when you are already top of the league, but it should be easy if your organisation is near the bottom.

In manufacturing organisations, improving means taking existing products and existing markets and finding ways of producing, distributing and selling that are more cost effective. It means tapping the existing market harder to get more 'market penetration' and it means greater productivity and better utilisation of assets.

Sometimes improvement is the only strategy a firm can pursue in the short run, since expansion and diversification demand greater resources than the very weak firm can get hold of. Until it improves, it cannot afford to expand or diversify, and no one will lend it money.

The key to improvement lies in the internal strengths and weaknesses appraisal which has already been looked at in Chapter 3. The biggest advantages of pursuing such a strategy are that it can be set under way quickly, it is cheap, it is easily quantified and is within the complete control of management. Unfortunately it has a weakness which makes it unsuitable in the long run as the only strategy to pursue. The weakness is that improving existing operations will not prevent the ultimate downward curve of performance because it is doing nothing to adapt products or services to meet the changing environment. All that improvement does is partly fill the gap.

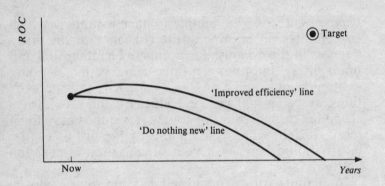

The importance of improvement as a strategy can be seen in three different situations:

- The very poor firm has to improve before anything else just to survive.
- The middle-of-the-road organisation needs to improve so that its weak points do not hamper its other strategies.
- The good organisations need to improve to stay on top.

In the first two cases the strategy is predominant for two or three years until performance is at a suitable level to support expansion.

The Case of Daisy Cycles Ltd

There was once a bicycle shop called Daisy Cycles. It had been around as long as anyone could remember but it had become dingy and unexciting. Very few customers came in to buy cycles – most sales were of accessories like bells and lamps, and repair work which was cheap. Cash was never plentiful, so the stock of bikes was never very high, so few customers came in. One day the owner retired and his son gave the shop a coat of paint and turned a corner of it to fishing equipment, using every penny he could lay his hands on. The business closed down just over a year later.

Why did it fail and what should the son have done?

Every new venture takes time to get off the ground. The trouble with Daisy Cycles was the lack of customers: not enough people knew about the diversification into fishing tackle. Moreover there was insufficient money for an adequate stock in that area. What cash there was from the cycle side of the business was diverted to fishing, leaving the cycle side even weaker. They borrowed to pay the bills, but little cash came in. In the end, the bank manager would not allow any more overdraft. The son should have concentrated his efforts, time and money on improving existing operations.

Expansion strategies. Expansion is a popular strategy to follow because it is fairly easy to get going and it keeps everyone busy. Strictly speaking expansion means one of two things in a business organisation: either it is taking the existing range of products and services and moving into a new market to try to increase their sales, or it is developing new products or services and trying to sell them in the existing market. Expansion is *not* a new product in a new market – that is diversification, which will be looked at in a moment. For now let's take a close look at these two types of expansion strategy.

Market expansion. Market expansion means the process of extending the area in which your business operates, so that more potential customers are aware of the products or services you are providing. The most obvious examples of this kind of activity are in the high street of your nearest town. There you will find several organisations represented that are also in every other high street in the country. The banks, for instance, are nearly always all to be found, as are various well-known shops like Boots, W. H. Smith and Marks & Spencer. Inside the shops the same products will be found over and over again. This repetition across the land stretches to insurance companies, building societies, garages dealing with a particular motorcar manufacturer and many more. This market spread has not occurred accidentally, nor simultaneously; it is the result of a deliberate decision on the part of the management of the company concerned to seek growth by this method.

Very often organisations cannot operate at full efficiency unless they are covering the whole of a region or country; it is not very effective to advertise your product on television if half your audience cannot buy your product. (A tiny proportion is probably acceptable, but half *is* wasteful.)

This kind of strategy has a number of advantages. First, it is fairly easy to implement. All you need is a team to go into the market and set the operation up. Second, the products or services being sold can easily be transferred from the existing locations, and the additional volume going through the system is a strong lever for more favourable prices from the suppliers: economies of scale again (see page 34). Third, the possibility of something going wrong is not very high because the services or products that are being offered are known to be acceptable in the market. Unfortunately this can sometimes backfire on a firm: just because your product is popular in Devon does not guarantee that it will be popular in Yorkshire. Moreover trying to expand across national frontiers can be very risky, as Marks & Spencer discovered when it first opened up a store in Paris: the way M&S operates in Britain in clothing (i.e. try it on at home, bring it back if it does not fit) was not in line with the custom in Paris. The whole operation nearly collapsed. A further problem with expansion geographically is that it becomes more difficult to keep an eye on what is happening. This is a particular problem for the independent retailer who opens his first branch. This issue will be examined again later.

A more subtle form of market expansion occurs not geographically but where it is realised that only a proportion of the population who could buy the product in fact do buy it. For instance, in America research was carried out seeking ways of increasing the consumption of prunes. It was discovered that most people regarded the product as something to be eaten only as a mild laxative. The product was subsequently promoted as an alternative dessert to more usual fruit, in an attempt to capture a different market segment.

Product/service expansion. Some organisations prefer to expand by adding to the list of products or services they are selling rather than to expand the territory in which they operate. The underlying idea is that by offering customers a wider range of products there is a better chance of them buying your products rather than your competitors'. Good examples of this are to be found in the food industry, especially in confectionery where new chocolate products arrive on the scene regularly, and in the frozen food business, with new frozen meals being introduced.

The advantages of this kind of expansion are that the new product can easily be added on to the firm's list of products; no separate sales force is needed, nor special distribution facilities, and no different paperwork. The chances of success should be high, since the company should know its market.

Unfortunately, new products are often expensive to develop. The collapse of Rolls-Royce in the early 1970s can be largely attributed to the huge cost of developing a new aero-engine, the RB211. Even developing an attractive new bar of chocolate costs money.

Moreover set-up costs can be high if extra plant and machinery is required, and the cost of launching the product, in terms of advertising and sales promotion, can be very high. To recoup the heavy outlay in getting the new product off the ground it has to sell extremely well, but there is no guarantee of success, no way of being certain the new baby will thrive. In fact the 'death rate' of new products in the consumer goods industries is very high. Estimates suggest that as many as eight out of every ten new products are abandoned soon after their introduction, and large numbers never reach the shops.

> Most people from time to time try something new and find it unacceptable, either because it is far too expensive, because it does not do the job it should or because it breaks down and cannot be repaired. Possibly the worst is the product which (through colour, smell or taste) makes you throw it away instantly. My own favourite disaster was a blueberry-flavoured breakfast cereal, which not only turned the milk blue but actually turned the children off cereals for a while.
>
> Look out for other disastrous products.

Diversification. To diversify is the only way to fill up the gap available to organisations which are efficient and which have expanded their markets and products as far as possible. This is because there is no limit to the amount of diversification that can be undertaken in the long term. Diagrammatically the alternative basic strategies look like this:

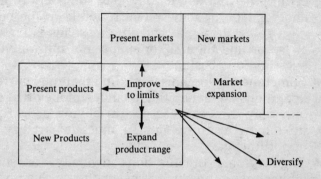

Put simply, diversification is doing something different – not in place of existing products and markets, but in addition.

There are several reasons why organisations choose to diversify:

- It may be the only reasonable way of filling the 'planning gap'. If your market is the world, your product range is comprehensive and you are efficient, then you have to diversify.
- It may be a better alternative than expansion. There are situations when to expand a market or the range of products is so expensive and the potential benefits are so small that it would not help much to expand in either direction; to achieve the required increase in performance needs diversification. For example, a company selling its products throughout Europe may look at North America as a potential market. The cost of getting into that

market would be very high and the risk of failure very great.

■ Diversification can be an insurance policy. If an organisation thinks that its existing operations are subject to an unacceptable level of threat from the environment, then it may put some effort into another type of activity which will keep the business going if the old activity dies. This is known as 'spreading the risk' or simply not putting your eggs into one basket.

■ Sometimes the organisations find that their current operations are generating so much money that the only way they can use it is in buying or starting up a new venture: not so much a strategy as opportunism.

■ Finally some organisations diversify for some whimsical reason, such as being offered a company which had some appeal to the management. This is diversifying 'just for the hell of it'.

Types of diversification. At one extreme, diversification can appear to be a logical extension of an organisation's current activities. *Reader's Digest* magazine also publishes books – the market is similar (but not the same), the product is similar (but not the same), and the techniques used in all stages are similar.

Then there is the kind of diversification seen in the case of Ford, manufacturing motorcars and tractors. The products and markets are different; the similarity is in the technology.

At the other extreme there is the sort of diversification where everything is different; no similarities exist at all. This is normally called 'conglomerate' diversification and an excellent example of this is the Pearson Group which owns, or has a substantial stake in, such diverse activities as:

- Newspapers (*Financial Times*)
- Waxworks (Madame Tussauds)
- A zoo (Chessington)
- Pottery (Royal Doulton)
- Book publishing (Longman and Penguin)
- A vineyard (Château Latour)

and many others.

A further type of diversification is what is known as 'vertical integration', meaning getting involved in a business commercially connected with your own. For example, a book publishing house may buy a printing firm, or even an ink works; and it may also open up bookshops to sell its products. The great advantage of this kind of arrangement is the control of supplies and the fact that profits stay inside the business all along the line.

In the example of Daisy Cycles (page 89), the bold venture into fishing tackle failed because the organisation was too weak.

It was suggested that if an improvement strategy had been followed the firm would not have collapsed. By moving into fishing tackle from bicycles, the shop was following a strategy of conglomerate diversification because the product technology is completely different and the market (although geographically the same) is completely different too. There might be a little overlap (i.e. cycling fishermen) but there is no other natural connection.

Would such a move make sense later? Possibly if we consider such factors as fishing: an increasingly popular leisure activity; it can be very profitable; it would spread the risk; it would utilise space effectively and spread the shop overhead costs. On the other hand, these favourable points have to be balanced against such factors as the high cost of getting into the business; the lack of knowledge of the business; the uncertainty: *will it be a success?*

There is no clear-cut answer to this; a great deal depends on whether we would be prepared to take a chance. If money is too precious to risk then it goes into the bank. If any risk is acceptable then the money can be put on a hundred to one racehorse in the Grand National. Between these two extremes lies the level of acceptable risk each organisation is prepared to tolerate. (More on this in Chapter 10.)

One further element that helps to make the decision easier is known as 'synergy'. Sometimes this is called the '2 + 2 = 5 effect', and it has been developed in a management sense by Igor Ansoff.* It is the idea that if two activities are put together, the outcome is a much better result than if they had been working apart. With conglomerate diversification there is usually very little synergy, whereas most synergy is experienced in expansion strategies. For instance, when two organisations merge, the combined research function has far better results than the independent units.

However, there can also be a negative synergy (2 + 2 = 3). This can happen in any strategy, but particularly where the new activity is bought (through a takeover for instance) rather than developed from within. The merger of the British car firms to form British Leyland resulted in negative synergy, and there have been many more.

Synergy can only come from strengths within the business; it cannot cure a weakness. It is like the effect of yeast on flour and water – without it the compound is not very palatable, but add it and good bread can result. The only difficulty is that synergy cannot be purchased on its own.

* In his book *Corporate Strategy* – see 'Further reading'.

Last words on strategy

The choice of strategy depends partly on the size of the planning gap. It also depends on the strengths and weaknesses of the organisation, and on the threats and opportunities seen to be in the environment. This evaluation is nowadays referred to as S W O T and, coupled with an understanding of the constraints placed on it, forms the basis of the search for a strategy to secure the long-term objectives of the organisation.

There is a lot to be said for the approach known as 'widening the search', i.e. looking for an opportunity close to one's existing operations that builds on a strength and offers some synergy. If there is nothing suitable, look further afield, and so on until the requirements of the gap have been met.

An alternative approach, popular some years ago, was to ask the question, What business are we in? The answer provides the clue to where to look for new opportunities. The difficulty with the question is that too broad an answer (e.g. We are in the money-making business) is useless; too narrow an answer (We sell bicycles) provides no ideas at all, and a middle answer (We are in the transport equipment business) can lead to odd diversification moves with no synergy (the bicycle shop starting a taxi service). Once chosen, a strategy involving expansion or diversification can be implemented by growth from within the firm, or can be achieved by taking over or buying up another company. The choice is governed by time and cost. The home-grown system is slower and cheaper; acquisition is quicker and more expensive.

What about strategies for departmental managers? Normally improvement is the only option to consider, but there are times when it is appropriate to seek to expand the department's acitivities and even diversify. This might be thought of as empire-building, but if the new activity could make a contribution to the overall objectives of the organisation, it must be considered.

6 The Structure of Companies

'Structure' is the jargon word for the way in which a company is organised internally. As companies grow and develop, their structure changes, sometimes slowly and easily, at other times suddenly and with far-reaching consequences. 'We've been reorganised . . . again' is a common cry and is often the result of a strategic decision taken at a corporate level in the business. Clearly, to succeed, a firm needs to be set up in the best way, so that effort and expertise are put in positions where they can be most effective. If, for instance, your traditional market area is Scotland and you decided to expand into England, you would use some of your best sales people; it would be necessary to restructure the sales force.

The decision to reorganise is one which never leaves many businessmen, for no sooner has a change taken place than a new set of circumstances crops up to alter things again. In this chapter we track the development of a firm from birth through all stages of its growth, to show how it needs to change if it is to grow and prosper.

The new organisation

Consider, first, the situation of a company that has just come into being as an independent concern; maybe where someone has decided to 'go it alone' and start out in business, or it could be where a relative takes over an old firm. Even at the start, it is highly unlikely that the owner will be operating entirely alone; the advice and help from such experts as solicitors and accountants will be used. These people are not paid staff but advisors and, as such, paid fees. Usually they are described as 'professional services'. They are services which organisations can never do without, although many firms do not employ accountants of their own until they have reached a considerable size and are quite big before they have their own legal experts.

The owner of the very small business has to be a jack-of-all-trades at first in the sense that he has to be able to turn his hand to any and every aspect of the business. Soon, in a small shop, it is likely that he will employ one or two sales assistants, often part-timers, and a small practical businessman such as a plumber or jobbing builder will often employ a 'mate' – someone to do the general, unskilled work. The owner's own job is a mixture of tasks, including buying, selling, pricing, housekeeping, display and carrying out the basic book-keeping activities that are needed to keep the money side of the business in order. Very often this last job is not considered sufficiently important to warrant the owner spending his time on it, and it is therefore common to find in such firms a part-time book-keeper employed too. The organisation chart of a small independent shop may look like this once it has got going.

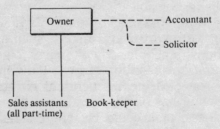

Other small firms will have a similar appearance, although instead of assistants on the selling side there will be assistants in other functions. For instance, in the case of a small firm of solicitors or estate agents, the first employee to be taken on will probably have general clerical or secretarial skills. Similarly, a small engineering workshop might usefully employ a skilled welder or general labourer.

The need to take on staff can arise for any number of reasons. In the organisation chart shown above, there could be several reasons for employing two part-time sales assistants and a book-keeper. For example:

- laziness (Not an attribute of a successful manager)
- the job is boring
- it is too time-consuming
- the owner does not have the expertise to do that particular task
- 'there are only twenty-four hours in the day and the job needs thirty-three'
- 'my time is better spent selling (or making) than typing'
- 'the business is growing too fast for me to cope on my own'.

Similarly, there are several good reasons for not hiring staff, including the obvious point that nobody hires assistance if the business is not making any money. Moreover, some small businessmen prefer not to have to be responsible for staff in any way, preferring a complete do-it-yourself approach. This in turn can come about for a variety of reasons, such as difficulty in getting on with people, unwillingness to get involved in all the legal aspects of hiring staff, and also an inability or fear of delegating work to somebody else.

Paying more wages and making more profit

Consider a greengrocer's shop on a Saturday morning. Nearly always there is a queue of people waiting to be served; some potential customers, seeing the queue, will not wait but will go elsewhere to buy their goods. If the shopkeeper had employed another sales assistant, the queue would have been shorter and he would have got the business that did not wait. The questions he has to resolve are, How many extra customers will I get if I hire another sales assistant? And, will the extra profit pay the extra wages and leave some over for me?

Fortunately there is a useful, simple technique for solving this kind of problem; it is called 'queueing theory' (surprise, surprise).

Another similar situation crops up where the owner feels his time would be more profitably spent in some other activity. For example he may, like the owner of Daisy Cycles, be both selling cycles and repairing them. If he does both, then every time a customer comes into the shop, the repair work stops and gradually less and less work gets done. The owner has to decide which activity he himself can most profitably carry out, and employ someone else to do the other work. Then he has to answer the question, Will I pick up enough extra work to pay for the extra wages and make me more money? If he does not feel happy trying to solve this problem, then he should ask his accountant.

The settled small organisation

Once the owner of a small organisation has recovered from the excitement and worry of hiring his first employee, it is not difficult for the total number of people employed to rise quite quickly up to the point where the business could not support any more growth. By now the owner is acting in a proper managerial role, leaving a large part of the routine operations to his staff, and the organisation structure may look as below for a large shop.

The important point as far as this, and all other simple organisations, is concerned is that all the staff report to one manager only, who is the owner or sole working director. None of the staff have any responsibilities of a managerial nature, all decisions are taken by the 'boss'.

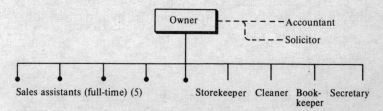

There are two important variations on this theme, the first being the small firm which is employing technicians or technical experts. Again all decisions are taken by the owner. Each technician is given work to do and may have assistants to do the routine work. This kind of firm is found in, for example, a technical drawing office or a central heating repair firm.

The second variation is the partnership where two or three individuals have come together to develop a business idea. Decisions tend to be taken collectively, but, apart from that, each partner often concentrates on his own area of specialisation – see illustration overleaf.

An organisation like this can be very strong if the partners understand and support each other's actions and aspirations but it depends for its success on effective and frequent communications. The disadvantage is that differences of opinion may slow down the decision-making process too much. The one-man operation can move much quicker because he does not have

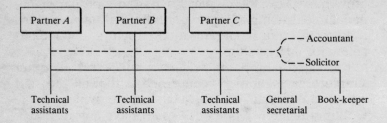

to consult or discuss – although the decisions he takes may not be as good as those reached by a partnership.

The divided business

Look back at the first organisation chart on page 100, showing how a large independently owned shop might be structured. Suppose that the business was so successful that the owner decided to open a similar shop in the next town ten miles away. How is he now going to manage both shops?

Once a business like this has decided where it is going to locate its second centre of operations, the question of managing both becomes critical, simply because the owner cannot be in both places at once. The three basic choices are: first set up both establishments in exactly the same way and travel to and from each one, keeping an eye on things all the time.

The owner would, of course, have his office at *A* along with the clerical and book-keeping functions. However because *B* is the new unit, most time would be spent away from *A* especially in the early months. So who would handle all the telephone inquiries and the sales representatives from supplier companies? To avoid this complication most small firms will take the

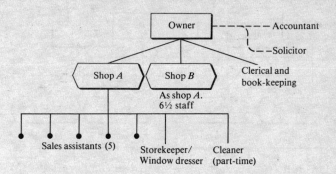

critical step of appointing either one or two managers. It is not an easy decision to take for the first time, because the owner thinks that he is giving away some of his personal power; he is trusting someone else with the business he built up, and he is in effect cutting himself off from the 'action' and possibly from some old friends. It has to be done, because there is no way of keeping track of everything that is going on in the organisation. The owner's effective span of control was the seven or eight people on one site, not fifteen people on two sites ten miles apart.

These two further possibilities are illustrated overleaf.

The better of these two solutions would be the second, to appoint a manager in charge of each shop. However, here there is a practical difficulty: who is to be appointed manager at each location? The success of the business in the future may well hang on these appointments, so it is important to get it right. Possibly the best answer would be to promote two of the existing staff to the new managerial positions. This would have the big advantage that they would know the owner, his values and beliefs and there would be no settling-in period. To be able to achieve this very desirable state of affairs needs considerable foresight.

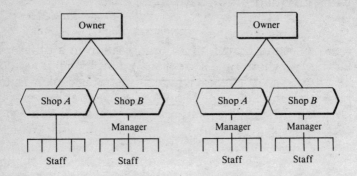

Delegation: the inevitable step

The moment the owner of a small business appoints a manager, he gets involved in delegation of a much more significant nature than before. All delegation is concerned with assigning tasks to subordinates; this is not difficult if the subordinates are close by, and their work is visible and easily controlled. However the act of appointing a manager involves delegating some authority and decision-making power.

This is hard for the owner and could also be dangerous. It is hard because, as we saw, he is cutting himself off. It is dangerous because the owner has to trust the manager to do the job properly.

At this stage in the development of the organisation the delegation of managerial responsibility can be the start of its success – or the beginning of the end; it all depends on who is appointed and how well he is trained.

More divided organisations

The example described above relates to a decision to open a second branch of an organisation in a different location. A shop was used for the example, but it would be any type of activity where the strategic plan is to grow by market expansion on a geographic basis. Dividing up an organisation is often referred to by the cumbersome expression 'departmentation', which simply means the process of splitting the business into departments. There are many different ways of doing it, and it is worth having a look at some of the main ones (this list will also apply to the problem of dividing work up between individuals).

Geographically. This is one we have just been considering and is obviously useful where it is important to be close, physically, to the territory in which the organisation wants to operate. For instance, a company based in Britain may consider that its market is the whole of Western Europe. Rather than attempting to do everything from its head office it may divide up the sales function (and later the production function), placing a separate operation in each country, or cluster of countries.

By function. In a manufacturing organisation the main functions of the business are production and sales. It is not uncommon to find, in a very small business, that the first manager to be appointed by the owners is either the sales manager, or a manager in charge of 'operations'.

One function not easily recognised by most small businessmen is that of marketing, as opposed to sales. Very often decisions regarding the marketing mix are taken by the owner without realising that they are really marketing issues and without the appropriate knowledge. A common trap is to first have a sales manager and then call him a marketing manager without either person really appreciating what marketing actually involves. It is best to recognise both functions early.

By product. As organisations grow, so the range of the products or services they are offering grows. At first all the products are handled using common facilities, but there comes a time when the volume being dealt with is so big that advantages are to be gained by treating each product as a separate company. For instance the Unilever organisation's soap powder operations (i.e. Lever Brothers) and its ice-cream business (i.e. Walls) are separate companies operating almost entirely on their own. In a department store, the products are divided up into departments because of the importance of specialised knowledge in both buying and selling.

By customer. This is particularly common in the selling function where it is felt that different kinds of customers require different treatment. This is particularly common in the food manufacturing industry where there is a distinction between the small independent shop and the large multiple supermarket firm. Each needs to be approached in a different way.

By process. Many operations, both clerical and in manufacturing, are performed in sequence, and it is one of the features of organisations that the sequences have tended to be split up into more and more smaller parts. The reason for this is that each separate process requires special skills; by specialising in a limited range of work, the operator becomes highly efficient, thus raising his productivity.

To pursue this kind of departmentation to its logical conclusion would result in all kinds of absurdity. Imagine what would happen if the work of bus drivers was divided up. Driver *A* would start up the bus, driver *B* would then take the bus out on to the road, where driver *C* would take over. Driver *D* would take control on dual-carriageway roads only and driver *E* would be used for stopping the bus. One could even imagine a situation where yet another individual, *F*, would stop the engine.

The absurdity of the example comes about because it is such an inefficient way of driving a bus. But a more serious issue lies beneath the surface, namely how do you think the people involved feel? Would they feel a bit frustrated at not being able to do the whole job?

By numbers. This system is used in, for instance, the army and in other circumstances where many people are required to carry out similar work to each other.

Alphabetically. A common way of dividing up work which is of a similar nature is on an alphabetic basis. This is particularly common in offices where large volumes of similar material have to be processed. One department will deal with all customers whose last names begin with the letters A, B or C. Another department handles D, E and F and so on.

Which sort of division to choose

It must be recognised that each way of dividing up an organisation has its advantages and disadvantages. Some methods are obviously completely unsuitable for the task. For instance, to divide up the management of British Rail alphabetically by name of station would be pointless. The key questions to ask include:

- Does the division tie in with overall strategies?
- Does it cost more than any other method?
- How easy will it be to coordinate the separate parts?

- Could it lead to interdepartmental battles? (Not avoidable in any split-up, but some are potentially more likely to result in war than others.)
- Are the members of the team likely to be motivated by the arrangement or not?

How many subordinates?

On page 105 we introduced the phrase 'span of control' with reference to the number of people working directly for the owner of a small shop. The phrase has been in use in management literature for a long time, although a more apt phrase would be 'span of management' since the idea behind it is not just concerned with control but with all aspects of managing. The question of how many subordinates a manager can handle is one which has taxed all kinds of people for a very long time.

The growing complex organisation

Eventually an organisation that has successfully divided itself up on a simple basis, such as we have been looking at, will find itself with another problem that comes about as it grows. The problem is known by the phrase 'chain of command'. This can best be illustrated by another example, that of a firm selling herbal bath-salts that decided to expand its sales force so that every chemist's shop in Britain would be visited once every two weeks. They calculated that they needed a total of 2,160 salesmen to do the job properly. Bearing in mind the problem of the span of control, they proposed creating a structure illustrated overleaf.

In other words, the chain of command had seven levels.

By being a little more flexible, and deciding that

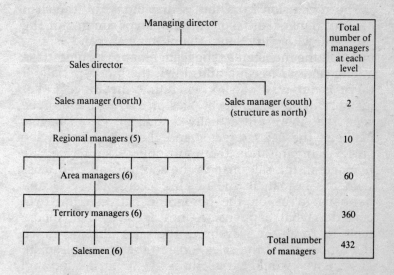

twelve salesmen could be comfortably managed by one manager, a revised structure was drawn up with only six levels:

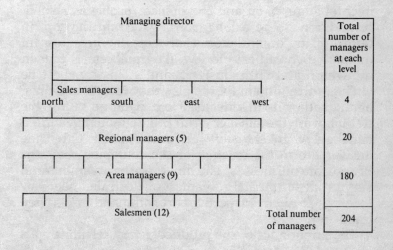

The conclusion from this is that the wider the span of management, the shorter the chain of command. The problem with very long chains of command is that instructions, questions, suggestions and requests take a long time to pass up and down the line especially if there is no way of short-circuiting the process. For instance in our seven-level salesforce structure it can be seen that there are actually a total of 432 managers between the sales director and the salesmen (in the six-level organisation there are only 204 intermediate managers). If a salesman in the south wants to discuss with a salesman in the north a client whose factory happens to be on the borderline between the two, consider what happens. A message would in theory have to go all the way up to the sales director, down the other side of the sales force to the other salesman. His answer would go all the way up to the top and back down the other side to the original salesman. No less than eighteen separate communications would have occurred; highly wasteful of time, energy and money.

The shorter the chain of command, the faster decisions are taken and the quicker problems solved. In addition, to be a long, long way from the top, in terms of an organisation chart, results in a loss of morale – people begin to feel like numbers or 'cogs in the wheel' and rather insignificant.

The problem then, for the growing, complex organisation is how to divide itself up without losing the flexibility of the smaller firm and without creating a situation where the staff feel unimportant. Often the answer lies in the creation of self-contained divisions or separate businesses. The difference between this and simple departmental organisation can be seen by looking at their respective organisation charts (see opposite).

The importance of the product/factory relationship is

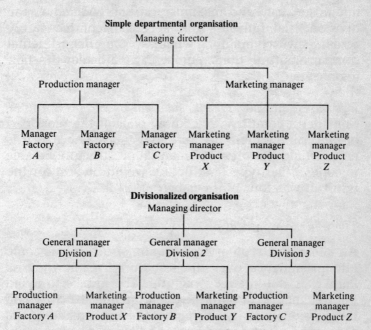

Simple departmental organisation

Managing director

Production manager   Marketing manager

Manager Factory A — Manager Factory B — Manager Factory C — Marketing manager Product X — Marketing manager Product Y — Marketing manager Product Z

Divisionalized organisation

Managing director

General manager Division 1 — General manager Division 2 — General manager Division 3

Production manager Factory A — Marketing manager Product X — Production manager Factory B — Marketing manager Product Y — Production manager Factory C — Marketing manager Product Z

that factory A would make product X; factory B would make product Y and factory C would make product Z.

In the divisionalised organisation the managing director is no longer concerned with coordinating the marketing and production functions of all the different products and factories. He has delegated that responsibility to each of the three general managers. His role can now be much more strategic in emphasis and concerned with the overall performance and prospects of each division as a separate business.

There are however some limitations to the divisional structure. It is not an appropriate structure for single-product companies, however large. It could lead to under-utilisation of some productive resources; the advantage of the departmental company is its ability to minimise waste and maximise capacity. Moreover the divisionalised business can spread talent too thinly across the company, whereas the departmental company puts all the expertise in a particular function together.

Two important, but difficult, questions
Consider a company you know well. If the workload of the firm suddenly became four times as big as it is now, would the present organisation structure be able to cope? What type of structure would be best for the firm if it was four times as big?

The matrix organisation

An alternative type of organisation structure has come into prominence over the last thirty years which is known as the 'matrix structure'. The idea is to avoid the weaknesses of both the departmental structure and the divisionalised structure we have just considered. Its roots can be found in advertising agencies, construction companies and in civil and aeronautical engineering firms, indeed it can be encountered in all types of organisations which are engaged in projects – i.e. activities with a specific limited objective. It can, however, be used in more standardised forms of activity too.

The essence of a matrix structure is that the functional relationships within the business still stand. For example there would still be a production manager with three factory managers reporting to him as in the top chart on page 113. However each factory manager would have a direct relationship with his counterpart on the marketing side, rather than an informal indirect contact. Using the charts on page 113, the matrix organisation structure is shown opposite.

Each marketing manager would take on a coordinating responsibility for his particular product, making

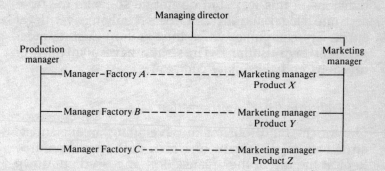

sure that all aspects of its production, distribution, storage, promotion and sale were handled in the most efficient and profitable way. Similarly in companies engaged in project work, a project manager would be appointed to make sure that the project was a success. He would have a number of experts reporting to him as long as the project was in progress, and as soon as it finished all concerned would move on. In the same way advertising agencies have account executives to manage each client company's advertising needs.

The holding company

Ultimately an organisation grows so large that the only effective way it can be managed is by making separate companies out of existing divisions. This can be done in such a way that the only relationship between each operating company and the top of the organisation is the legal one of ownership, the divisions becoming 'wholly owned subsidiary' companies. The actual connections become mainly concerned with the movement of finance and the transfer of profits, and the head office management interfere only if adequate profits are not being generated.

Many big organisations operate self-contained

divisions in this way, but do not go so far as to create separate legal entities. Others only have legal subsidiary companies when they buy up existing independent organisations. Thus they have a mixture of divisions and subsidiary companies.

Centralisation v. decentralisation

One of the big problems in developing organisational structures is the extent to which authority should be kept at the top of the organisation or passed out down the line. In effect this implies that if all decisions are taken by the owner of a small business, or by the managing director of a larger organisation, then it may be described as a highly centralised operation. On the other hand if the power to take decisions is passed away from the top, then it is a relatively decentralised organisation. As we have seen, the owner of the small firm has to delegate; and the more he delegates, the more his firm is decentralised.

If the organisation charts on pages 113 and 115 fairly represent actual authority then it is easy to see that the departmental organisation is still centralised, while the authority in the divisional company is passed down a level from the managing director to the general managers of each division. Similarly in the matrix structure, the authority must be decentralised to the project team leader if that kind of structure is to work effectively.

The line and staff problem

Early in the chapter we looked at the professional services that a small firm might hire for specific jobs. We also brought into the picture a part-time bookkeeper. All these services are essential yet they are not at all directly connected with the production, distribution and marketing of the organisation's goods or services. They are like the umpires, coach, groundsmen and scorers at a cricket match: not actually in the game, but essential to its success. All organisations have to have the services of a variety of experts and, as they grow, so they bring in more and more such people. These areas of expertise are usually referred to as 'staff functions'.

The accountancy function is one of the most important of these because every transaction that the organisation makes has to be recorded and checked. In addition, the enormous sums of money flowing through companies (even the smallest) need to be carefully controlled. Finally many decisions in organisations are related (or at least should be) to improving efficiency and effectiveness and the accountancy function is best placed to help managers arrive at a good decision. The accountant does not make the product, nor does he sell it, but without his expertise the organisation would very soon collapse.

Similarly the need for experts in personnel, legal and company-secretarial, buying, market research, statistics and a hundred other areas is vital for the continuing success of the firm as it grows.

In contrast, the makers and the sellers in an organisation are known as 'line functions', because their authority is received straight 'down the line' in the chain of command.

Decentralising staff functions

The discussion on decentralisation on page 116 was in relation to the line functions of an organisation. However a separate problem exists with staff functions, because they can easily remain centralised while the operating parts of the organisation are decentralised.

The following simplified organisation charts illustrate the dilemma:

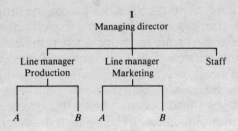

This departmental organization may change to either of these two structures:

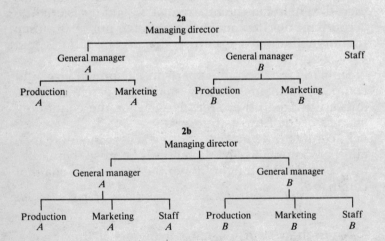

The issue is: should staff continue to report directly to the top when the line responsibilities are being decentralized (2a) or should they be decentralized too (2b)? The problem can be seen at its clearest in relation to the buying function, namely: centralized buying or not?

Some large diversified organisations insist on a highly centralized buying function – a group of skilled buyers operating from the headquarters of the organisation and making purchases for the group of companies as a whole. Other organisations have merely a token buying function at head office, leaving all the work to buyers at the level of the subsidiary company or division. At the local level decisions can be made quickly, sudden problems can be quickly solved and the buyer has a better knowledge of the needs of the operating managers in the division. He will not, however, have the power and leverage that a headquarters buyer can exert. So what does the company do?

Each organisation has to choose whether or not to decentralize its staff functions unless they are so specialized that it is obviously uneconomic to duplicate them across all parts of the organisation. There is no right or wrong answer to this: it all depends on the needs of the organisation.

How does an organisation's structure change?

Structure depends on:

- *the type of business or activity*
- *size*
- *strategies*
- *policies*
- *the values of the people in positions of power in the organisation*

Organisation structures are changing all the time as new opportunities arise, as old activities die away, and as the organisation itself develops and grows. Most of the time the structure changes gradually, but every so often it is necessary, for a variety of reasons, to have a radical reorganisation. As one expert on organisation development called it, 'Evolution and Revolution as

Organisations Grow'.* There are many reasons why these reorganisations take place; these do not concern us here. It is enough to note that companies do change; they grow and prosper or wither and die. There is, however, nothing to say that they have to die. Certainly, though, if they fail to adapt their structures to meet the requirements of new strategies and new circumstances their chances of success will be diminished.

* Title of an article by Larry E. Greiner in *Harvard Business Review*, July–August 1972.

7 Policies in Marketing and Sales

We look here at the key areas of choice all firms face in the marketing and sales functions. It will quickly become apparent that the two functions are not the same, although some firms seem to think that marketing is just a smart name for selling: it is in fact a very different animal. To illustrate the scope of marketing, consider the following case example of an unsuccessful soft-drinks firm:

THE CASE OF THE FIZZO SOFT DRINKS COMPANY

Ten years ago the Fizzo Soft Drinks Company was a run down old-established soft drinks firm in Scotland. The owner died, leaving the company to a distant relative who decided to put his savings into the firm and build up the business. He found that the products were tasty, the sales force were able (although they were only two in number) and the rest of the staff were loyal and keen to help in the development of the firm. The factory was entirely rebuilt on modern lines with brand-new up-to-date equipment. In total, fifteen different flavours of 'pop' were produced, all of it put in large glass bottles with a screw-top cap.

New delivery vans were purchased (and carefully painted with the ancient livery of the firm on the side). However, sales remained static and only went up whenever there was a heatwave, which was not all that often.

The overall effect was depressing because the bottling plant had finished production by lunchtime each day, and most afternoons were spent keeping the place cleaned and well maintained. In a nutshell, a lot of money had gone out and very little had come in. So the new owner called a meeting of the two salesmen, the accountant, the bank manager and two or three older and more senior employees.

The problem of the firm was easily identified as not enough bottles of pop being sold. The underlying problem was, How do we increase sales?

The ideas that emerged for raising sales of soft drinks included:

1 Sell more flavours.
2 Put the products into plastic bottles.
3 Put the products into small bottles or cans.
4 Advertise heavily.
5 Employ more salesmen.
6 Redesign labels or packaging.
7 Cut prices.
8 Offer better terms to retailers if they buy in large quantities.
9 Run special promotions, e.g. 'Collect ten labels and receive an ice-bucket free.'
10 Find out more about the customers and what they want.

All ten suggestions made are possible ways of increasing the firm's overall sales, but some would have a much better chance of success than others. The problem for the owner was to decide how many of the ideas should be employed to increase sales.

To do all these things instinctively feels wrong; and indeed, for a small company not doing very well, to attempt everything might be disastrous, simply because of the drain on limited resources (it would cost a lot of money) and the risk of failure being relatively high.

Idea 10 is the joker in the pack because its adoption would not increase sales directly. It is simply an information-gathering activity which on its own cannot sell anything. It is, however, an important part of marketing – usually termed 'market research' and an early policy decision to be made by any organisation is how much (if any) effort should be spent on it. Market research can range from a very simple survey of, for instance, the number of shops in an area carrying a rival's products, to very sophisticated studies involving computer programs and many dozens of researchers asking questions of people in the streets. There is no rule of thumb to tell you how much market research to do; it all depends on how badly you need to know and how much you are willing to spend.

Ideas **1** to **9** are all variations on a theme – the marketing theme – and the preferred ranking of the nine (in order of best for the job) is given later in the chapter. Right now the focus has to be on the major areas of decision in the marketing function, which is the part of the business that links corporate strategy with day-to-day operations.

The key policy decisions in marketing and sales can be grouped together under a broad heading commonly called 'the marketing mix' and a convenient way of classifying the variables for which policies can be formulated is known as the 'four ps'. These are:

- product
- place
- promotion
- price

A successful marketing operation is one where the mix is working to best advantage, namely that the product is right, it is in the right place, at the right price and is promoted in the right way. Of the nine ways of increasing Fizzo's sales, the first three are product questions, the fifth is concerned with place; numbers 4, 6 and 9 are promotion matters (and so is 5 partly) and 7 and 8 relate to price. Each of the four 'Ps' can now be studied in greater depth.

'Product' policies

Quality. Any and every product or service offered for sale can be of high quality or low quality or just average. Every type of industry or trade or service seems to produce the equivalent of a Rolls-Royce at one end of the quality scale and a cheap shoddy product at the other end. To decide where on the scale a firm's products or services will be is a fundamental marketing policy decision, the word 'quality' meaning different things in different contexts. An airline may be well-known for the quality of its in-flight service; another, infamous for the lack of service.

Product range. There are very few firms that make or sell a single separate product. Even British Gas sells appliances and a maintenance service in addition to its main product, gas. Most firms find that it is easy, cheap and beneficial to offer the market a range of products or services so that there is a better chance of achieving a sale. So, for example, a bed-maker offers a range of beds of different size, but also of different quality too – so that different spending power will be attracted to the firm's products. Another example is the soft drinks firm that offers a range of flavours and possibly in different sized bottles.

This conveniently provides an illustration of the overlap that exists between a strategic decision and a policy decision. The strategic decision to expand by growth in the range of products or services offered sets the general tone of the firm's activities. It will be a decision that is arrived at with due regard to the marketing function's analysis of the markets. The policy decisions which follow are those concerned with the precise manner in which the expansion should take place. For instance, the first three ideas for increasing Fizzo's sales of soft drinks are all policy matters, then the statement can be made, 'Our policy is to seek product expansion by developing a parallel range of products to those in large bottles, but in smaller "mixer"-sized bottles as well.'

A variation on this theme is what is known as 'bolt-on extras' whereby customers can have a number of optional features added to the basic product if they want. The motorcar industry is the best-known example of this, as it is of another similar idea called 'custom design'. Here the customer has to decide on certain features which are added to a standard basic product, making it different from the rest in some way.

Finally, there is one other basic option in this respect – namely, not to make any 'standard' products at all, but to manufacture whatever the customer wants within the broad area of technical competence of the business. A printer can come into this category, if he decides to be a 'jobber' simply waiting for a printing job that may have no relationship with the last job.

The extent to which the company gets involved in these kinds of activities are very much key policy decisions.

Guarantees and after-sales service. All products from any reputable firm have some form of guarantee or warranty, and many products of a durable nature have some service arrangements built in to make sure that any faults are corrected without extra cost to the owner.

'Place' policies

In marketing terms 'place' has a very wide meaning. It not only refers to the basic question of the precise place where a customer can go to buy the product or the service, but includes issues such as the way in which the product is to be moved from the factory to the final selling point. Once the basic strategic decision has been taken defining the market in broad terms (territory to be covered), a whole range of alternatives have to be examined and decisions made about them. A set of rules in this area eliminates a considerable amount of debate and discussion.

Suppose that Fizzo has defined its overall market as Scotland; it now has to ask itself four very important questions, namely:

To whom are we actually going to sell our products? An organisation does not have to sell to the final consumer of the product. The soft drinks firm may sell bottles of lemonade directly to schoolboys, but it is not likely that it would rely on this form of activity to achieve the sales volume it wants. However in some contexts direct selling is probably the most appropriate method. Banks in effect sell direct and so do building societies mostly. Very few consumer products these days pass directly from manufacturer to consumer. It would however apply if a large order was being placed, and also in industrial markets where the product in question is sold by one firm to another firm to form part of its own product.

If it is decided that the customer (i.e. the person who buys the product) is not to be the final consumer the choice left is either:

- an agent; someone who finds customers for products and services, or who finds a product or service for a customer. Typically this kind of activity is found in exporting where a firm may decide that it is too expensive to set up a separate sales organisation in a particular country. By appointing an agent, in effect the firm is buying a ready-made expert.

Other examples of businesses that work through agents are to be found in the travel and tourist world, insurance, car distributors; or

- a wholesaler; someone who buys a range of products often in bulk, splits them up and sells to a large number of smaller customers. Newspapers and magazines typically are distributed in this way; or
- a retailer; someone who sells a range of products to final consumers.

The policy chosen may be to sell exclusively to one type of customer, or it may be decided to adopt a 'mixture' policy. This may well be necessary if the product itself is normally sold through many different channels. For instance there are at least six or seven different types of places where you could buy a bottle of bitter lemon (e.g. shop, supermarket, pub, club, off-licence, restaurant and hotel).

How do we get our products to our customers? Once the decision has been taken regarding who the customer will be, the next decision is related to the method used to get the products to the customer. The choice is usually between the simple method of sending the goods direct from production unit to customer or by sending the products to warehouses or stores located in suitable places.

The factors which will affect the choice include:

- distances involved
- the size of the loads
- extent to which the products are perishable
- and, of course, the relative costs of operating the two systems

A particularly difficult policy to formulate arises if the company decides to sell direct to the final consumer of the product. For instance it is highly improbable that Fizzo would choose to sell via mail order catalogues, nor would it sell through a chain of soft drink shops. It would have to send its vans out around the streets, in effect combining the functions of selling and physical distribution. This kind of door-to-door service used to be fairly common, but it is now limited to the occasional soft drinks firm and, in the summer, the ice-cream man.

The alternatives are all possible but for the soft drinks business not the wisest alternative – partly because of the cost of setting up the system and partly because it is difficult to see how such operations could be successful. It is unlikely that customers would bother to order their soft drinks on a mail-order basis, or go to a central warehouse to collect them when similar products could be bought at the shop around the corner. Moreover demand for soft drinks is not normally high enough to make an exclusive retail soft drink shop a viable proposition.

To what extent should we try to cover the market? This is a deceptively simple question. Suppose it is decided that the customer is the retailer and the product is therefore going to be sold in retail outlets only, the question to be resolved is, What proportion of all the retail outlets in the area are going to be asked to carry the goods? And, as a follow-up question, How often is each outlet going to be serviced (i.e. called on or phoned, or delivered to)? Cost and the pattern set by competition are key guides here, as is the desired level of service. Generally the nearer 100–per-cent coverage a firm aims at, the higher will be the average cost of a call.

What physical distribution system should we use? This issue is a straight choice between:

rail or
air or
sea or
road (own vehicles or hired vehicles or common carrier)

Once again there is no easy answer to this question. The policy chosen will depend on the product, the channel of distribution, distance, cost, level of service and the extent to which the firm wants to retain control over its products as they travel down-stream (literally and figuratively).

'Promotion' policies

Fizzo had an excellent range of products. The products were available widely throughout the area, yet sales failed to rise to a level sufficiently high for a decent return on the investment that had been made. If there had been no competition then the firm would have done well – there would be no choice.

There is, however, in the soft drinks business quite a lot of choice, and 'promotion' in the widest sense of the word is concerned with the whole issue of persuading the customer to choose one particular brand of product rather than another. In fact promotion goes on in all walks of life all the time, as people and institutions attempt to persuade others of the merits not merely of their products but of their services, their ideals, politics, beliefs and religions. So that whenever a politician stands up to speak, his aim is to promote himself, his party and its (or his) policies.

Similarly every manager and every organisation is concerned from time to time to get involved in promotion one way or another; the policy decisions being concerned with the extent to which promotion is carried out, and the precise way in which it is carried out.

Generally, promotion covers five elements:

- *advertising*
- *publicity*
- *selling*
- *sales promotion*
- *packaging*

and it is helpful if policies are established in each of these areas.

Advertising. The three key questions at the policy level, so far as advertising is concerned, are:

- What is the advertising going to say (the message)?
- How much is going to be spent?
- Where are we going to advertise (the medium)?

The message. The message can be almost anything and indeed marketing textbooks list dozens of different types of messages that can be contained in an advertisement. They range from the type that contains no words – merely a picture of the product in a particular location: for example, the bottle of beer in the desert sand – to, at the other end, the advertisement which is an essay persuading you of the merits of a particular product or service and includes a cut-out piece to send your name and address off either for a catalogue or to buy. The 'Become an officer in the Army' advertisement is of this type. The important thing is to be clear why advertising is taking place and when advertising will not be carried out.

What is the message? Study some of the advertisements in magazines or in the newspaper. You should be able to see what the advertiser is trying to tell you, but do not worry if you cannot see the message; advertisers sometimes fail to 'get the message across' and then they have simply wasted money.

How much to spend

There have to be some rules about this, otherwise no profits would be made at all since there is no obvious limit to the amount that can be spent. Theoretically, every additional £1 spent on advertising will generate extra sales. However, there is a point at which extra advertising expenditure yields no additional sales. Ideally, the amount spent on advertising should be just enough to ensure maximum profit; this ideal can never be reached – the old joke: Half the amount we spend on advertising is wasted; the problem is we do not know which half.

How much to spend, therefore, depends on how widely the message has to be spread; how much can be afforded and what the competition is doing.

The medium

There are many ways in which the advertising message can be passed on. For example, a complete list of possible ways of advertising soft drinks would include:

radio
television
cinema
newspapers
magazines
leaflets through doors
shop-window displays
sky writing
posters on buses
posters on hoardings
airships

The policy decision as to which medium to use emerges from an analysis of the market – what it is and what is the best way of reaching it.

Publicity. Publicity can be defined as free advertising, in that it means that the organisation concerned, or its products or services, gets its name mentioned in public without them having had to pay anything. This is now recognized as an important supplementary to advertising, and companies in fact take a lot of trouble to cultivate potential sources of free advertising. A brief interview on television about a new product or service can give a firm more exposure than it would get by spending £100,000 on an advertising campaign.

Some organisations shun publicity. Others welcome it and, through their public relations department, push out an endless stream of information about themselves. For instance, many annual reports of companies have been used directly as a source of quotations for this book.

Selling. Selling, in this context, is a meeting between a representative of the selling organisation and a potential buyer. It is usually face to face but can be conducted on the telephone. The word 'salesman' embraces a very wide range of activities, from someone who is little more than an order-taker, to someone who is trying to get new customers where none existed before, and to highly professional consultants whose job is to design a product for a customer as a one-off job.

The main policy decisions in this area relate to the precise use that should be made of sales people and this possibly will depend on such things as the type of product and the channels of distribution chosen. If the two extreme definitions of the word 'salesman' are taken it can be seen how this decision is closely tied up with some other fundamental operating policy decisions:

- The order-taker tends to be – selling from a catalogue; 'standard products'.

■ The technical adviser tends to be – custom-building; 'jobbing shop'.

It will be recalled that these product options were discussed earlier in the chapter under 'product policies' (page 124) and they will be met again later in the next chapter when operating policies are discussed.

Finally as regards sales people, a very important ground rule is the one relating to the way sales people are paid for the work they do. Many salesmen are given cars – an essential tool of the trade – but some receive a salary which is very low. This type of organisation pays its salesmen chiefly on a commission basis, giving them the chance to earn sometimes more than the highest paid director in the firm. Other firms pay generous salaries and relegate the idea of a commission or bonus to a minor place in the 'remuneration package'. The choice is the company's, depending on what it considers is the best way of attracting, keeping and motivating the best salesmen.

Sales promotion. Sales promotion activities can be directed either at the final consumers, persuading them to buy, or at retailers, persuading them to stock the products.

Sales promotion techniques are everywhere – coupons through the letter-box with 5p off a tube of toothpaste; buy ten and get a free sunshade; competitions; free samples and so on. Their use is to boost sales in slack periods, encourage customers to try a new product or to clear out a product which is just about to be replaced by a new one.

The danger with sales promotion activities is that they may cheapen the image of the product or the organisation, and thus may run counter to all its other policies. It has, therefore, to be used carefully – the initial policy decisions being, Do we use sales promotion techniques? If so, when, and which kinds?

Packaging. Packaging is an essential part of the 'promotion mix' in that it can be an important part of the fight to get the consumer to choose one brand as against another. There are two main policy considerations:

- Minimum standard or 'expensive' packaging (in both looks and in actual quality)?
- How frequently should the packaging design be updated?

Poor packaging can turn potential customers away – that is certain. How far the reverse is true is arguable.

'Pricing' policies

Whenever a product or service is made available for sale, one of the most important decisions is the one related to the price to be charged. To have no policy regarding price – merely to 'think of a number' – is to invite trouble because some products may seem cheap and some may seem expensive. As a result the market can get confused and not buy at all.

The basic decision as far as pricing is concerned is to answer the question, At what level should we pitch our prices? A relatively high price (in relation to the competition) indicates that the product has something special about it not found in the other products. In other words the customer is expected to pay a premium for the extra-special qualities to be found in the product. This also applies to services like any form of maintenance or repair work (garages, plumbers, electricians, etc.). Unfortunately it is a well-established economic law that the higher the price, the lower the volume sold. On the other hand, if your prices are low many more will be sold.

The extremes of pricing policy are the Fortnum & Mason type and the Tesco type. Fortnum's have the reputation of high quality and service, allied with high prices, but with low volume; whereas Tesco's have average quality and service, low prices and very high volume. Both ends of the market can be equally profitable.

A related policy decision is concerned with discounts. Some organisations offer discounts out of habit, others never give any kind of discount. In the food business, especially in the non-perishable part (e.g. canned food), it is common to offer a retailer extra discounts for buying in bulk, and the more he buys the bigger is his discount. This is known as a 'quantity discount'.

'Prompt-payment discounts' are another inducement to the customer (usually retailers), whereby if payment is made quickly (say, within ten days) the amount payable is a little less than it would normally be.

As far as a retailer is concerned he is particularly interested in the size of the difference between what he pays the manufacturer and what the customer pays him, i.e. the 'trade discount'.

Another important element in the decision is how payment is to be made. Why is it, for example, that Marks & Spencer do not accept Access cards or Barclaycard or American Express, whereas British Home Stores do accept them quite readily? Why is it that some organisations demand cash with order, yet others go for cash on delivery and some others do not demand payment until the end of the month? The answer to all these questions is that each organisation has decided on its payment policy; they have decided that their particular way of doing business is best.

Follow-my-leader. For the firm with a small market share,

especially where there are two or three very big firms and many small ones (like the soft drinks industry in Britain), one pricing policy decision that has to be made is whether to pitch prices and related terms at the same level as the 'big boys' or whether to go higher or lower. There are risks whichever is chosen, but regard to the other elements in the marketing mix helps to reduce that risk.

Fizzo Soft Drinks revisited

At the beginning of the chapter the situation of this soft drinks company was described, and its main problem was identified as, quite simply, that its sales volume was too low. Excluding the suggestion to carry out some market research, nine specific ideas were put

Ideas for raising sales	Marketing mix type	Comments
1 Sell more flavours	Product	Probably wide enough already
2 Use plastic bottles	Product	Good idea – if equipment will cope
3 Small bottles or cans	Product	
4 Advertise heavily	Promotion	Yes – but through which medium?
5 More salesmen	Promotion/place	Possibly for better coverage of existing territory
6 New labels	Promotion	Definitely
7 Cut prices	Price	Not if it means no more profit and same volume
8 Bigger discount to retailers for bulk buying	Price	Only if the present discount structure is a hindrance
9 Special sales promotions	Promotion	May be useful temporarily

forward for improving the volume of sales. The ideas in the list were classified according to the marketing mix categories which we have been considering. It is now possible to look again at each idea and comment on each, deciding which of all the alternative actions is best. Look at the table opposite.

So out of the nine suggestions, it is possible that 2, 3, 4 or 6 would rank highest, with 5 and 9 as a second level; 7 and 8 are possibilities only after some research; 1 is a last resort.

There are many other ideas that could be thought out to boost the sales of soft drinks, and indeed the sales of any product or service are capable of being increased by a considered marketing approach. To have sensible policies in this area – rules that fit the needs of the organisation – improves the chances of success significantly.

8 Policies in Buying and Operations

Most people in the West eat some bread every day. Most of us never give it a second's thought, but every time we take a loaf and eat a bit we have in fact carried out a process involving a whole string of decisions. For most of that process is automatic – we do not have to think about it – simply because some time ago we made ourselves some rules, some policy decisions, which we carry out now without any further thought.

The very first thing to decide on is whether to buy our bread requirements from the shop or make it ourselves. Maybe a compromise is reached and we decide to make a little bread at the weekend but to buy most of our needs most of the time. If we decide to make our own bread, several other decisions have to be taken before we can taste the results of our efforts. The most important are:

- How many different types of bread to make?
- What kind of flour to use?
- Which recipe(s) to follow?
- In what to mix the dough?
- Hand mixing or machine mixing?
- Where do we buy the ingredients?
- Do we buy more flour and yeast than we need for one bake?
- How much to make at a bake? (Enough for two days for example, or enough for two weeks – putting the rest in the freezer if we happen to have one?)
- What is the best form of oven heating for bread?

Similarly if we decide, on the whole, to buy our bread in the shops we have another set of decisions to think through:

- How much bread to buy at a time? (Again the question of freezer storage comes into the picture.)
- What sort of bread to buy?
- When to buy?
- From where do we buy bread?

There are not quite so many decisions to make as there are if we had decided to make our own bread. This should not be taken to imply that the decisions are easier; in many respects – as you will see – the decisions connected with buying can be extremely difficult.

It is possible to illustrate the decisions we have been looking at in simple diagram form – see overleaf.

Many of the problems that have been described in relation to an individual acquiring bread are broadly similar to those encountered by managers in all kinds of organisations. There are very few organisations that can get by without having to buy something from outside; possibly the occasional commune, kibbutz or monastery may be able to do-it-itself entirely but this is very rare.

Even problems relative to specific types of equipment do not only relate to the production and distribution functions; offices too have to think these things through carefully and develop policies to handle them. For the eighth problem in the office, change the words to, Which type of furniture/typewriters/data-processing equipment do we buy?

The primary problem of all – make or buy? – is there for every organisation no matter what its function. It is not an all-or-nothing decision usually, but more a question of degree: How far are we going to make things ourselves? In this context the word 'make' refers not only to products but also to services.

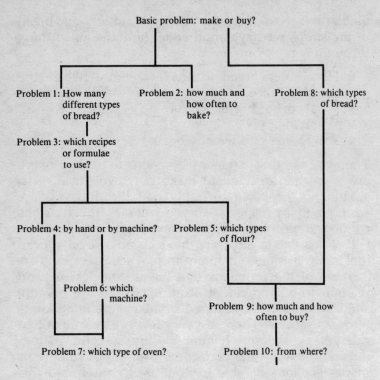

The decision 'Make or buy?' is a fundamental policy decision, so it will be examined first, looking at major issues in the areas of buying and operations later.

Marks & Spencer make nothing themselves; they buy all the goods they sell. Boots the Chemists manufacture some of the products they sell and buy other products from different makers. They could, in theory, make everything they sell in their own production units. Some firms in fact do make everything they sell all the way back to the production of the raw material – motorcar manufacturers making their own steel and power, for example.

As we have seen, the basic question all organisations have to ask is, Which is best: to buy the material, product, component or service from an outside supplier, or do it ourselves? To have to ask this question every month about everything bought out is very tedious and time-consuming. Instead organisations tend to have a fairly clear-cut policy on the subject. At one extreme there is the Marks & Spencer type policy of, 'Make nothing, just buy and sell.' (A similar policy is, 'Buy, stick on a label and sell.') And at the other extreme there is the firm which tries to do it all itself. When to have a 'make' policy:

- If your suppliers are unreliable (e.g. if they are inefficient, strike-prone, have variable quality in their work, or if they are overseas and liable to political interference).
- If you can make it cheaper than your suppliers can supply it (not so simple a calculation as you might think).
- If your firm has a competence in the technology (or can easily buy it). This is to pick up some synergy (see page 96 for a definition of this word).
- If the organisation is looking for an investment opportunity.
- If there is capacity (in space and in management).
- If control over the activity is essential.

When to have a 'buy' policy:

- If your own capabilities in producing the goods or services are weak (e.g. poor production facilities, no managerial experience, labour problems).
- If you can buy cheaper than you could make.
- If the cost of entry into the business is very high.
- If the suppliers are reliable and you can be sure of getting the level of service you require.
- If the future for the product is doubtful (for example, if you sell a 'craze' product like a skateboard it is risky buying the manufacturing facilities

too. You may be left with a lot of useless equipment).

Policies in operations

Once an organisation has taken the basic decision to make a proportion of the products or services it is providing, a number of other important policy decisions have to be established. These correspond roughly with the list of questions that was drawn up on page 138 to illustrate the issues that have to be resolved in making bread, although managers tend to use somewhat different words. The main decisions are:

How many different products to make?

This is the problem that has already been met both in relation to the development of a strategy of expansion, and in the analysis of the marketing mix. In managerial terms it is known as the size of the product range.

To make life easy for any manager in production (or indeed in any type of operation), it is undoubtedly best to provide one product or service only. To do so would raise productivity to its highest possible level. This is because everyone concerned would become highly expert and skilled at producing that particular article. Moreover since only one product was being made it would be unneccesary to adjust or clean equipment frequently, as is a common feature in multi-product works.

To illustrate this idea consider the bread-making example. If only one type of bread is made then it is only necessary to clean the equipment at the end of production for the day. If however the daily production is of five different types of bread, then equipment has to be cleaned five times each day. Nothing can be produced during cleaning times and output per man (the traditional definition of productivity) falls.

The effect is similar where machinery has to be modified for each different product. Industries where this is a problem include all those where the product is made by pouring a liquid into a mould, allowing it to cool into its final hard form: for example, glass bottles, many plastic products and many metal products (i.e. those made in iron or steel foundries). In all these and similar industries, the greater the number of products to be made, the greater the number of times the equipment has to be stopped so that dies and moulds can be changed. The greater the down-time for equipment cleaning, as it is called, the lower will be productivity and the higher will be the cost. A single product would, therefore, be ideal from an operations angle, but strategically and from a marketing point of view a single product operation is often a very weak and vulnerable business.

To reconcile these two views it is necessary either:

- to have such a large demand for each line that a separate production unit can be justified for each. Unfortunately only firms with very big demand can do this;
- or management has to try to find that point where profits are likely to be greatest. The marketing manager will state that the more products that can be offered, the greater will be the sales. In contrast, the operations manager will insist that the more products that are made, the lower will be average profit per unit.

Somewhere there has to be a compromise, and a clearly established rule in this area avoids much of the trouble that can arise in arriving at the compromise.

How much to make; how often?

Having decided the size of the product range, the second key decision hangs around quantities and timing. The alternatives can be classified as follows:

1 Make the products before the orders have been placed by the customers, in long production runs (to get productivity as high as possible) placing all production into store until sales get the orders. This is known as 'making to stock' or 'selling ex-stock', and has undoubted advantages so far as production planning, productivity and distribution planning are concerned. Also sales people find it handy to be able to offer the products on an immediate delivery basis.

Many firms operate in this way, particularly in the consumer goods industries. All the products seen in the shops are made 'in anticipation of demand' and the manufacturer by doing things this way is, hopefully, keeping costs down. He is taking a risk, however, because the products he has made may never sell; in which case he would lose a lot of money. On top of this any company engaging in this kind of activity finds that it has to pay out a lot of money (in wages and for the cost of materials) often months before the sale is made. Tying up money in this way (in big stock levels) can cost a lot – especially if the business has to borrow from the bank to keep stocks high. Nevertheless, it can and often does pay off.

A related example of this kind of activity is in bread-making where the baker has to make in anticipation of customer demand. He risks not selling enough or not being able to satisfy the demand; either way, an unsatisfactory state of affairs. He does not have to carry stock, which saves him money, but it can raise his wastage rates very high if he overproduces too often.

The bread-maker has to make each product daily because bread is so perishable. If the product is not perishable, nor likely to go out of fashion, then it can be made at any convenient time and stored. Therefore making in anticipation of demand can only be justified if you can be reasonably sure that there is likely to be a continuing demand for your products.

2 At the other end of the scale, rather than manufacture in anticipation of demand, a firm can choose to wait until the customer places an order. A good example of this would be in the manufacture of oil rigs. It is unlikely that many such objects are constructed for selling ex-stock – the cost of holding it unsold and the risks of not selling at all are much too high. Instead these costly constructions are made when the customer asks for them.

Supporting issues that have to be resolved in this area involve the crucial one of whether the products will be standard lines identifiable in a catalogue, or whether the whole production operation will be a jobbing shop; in other words being willing and able to make anything within a broad area of technical expertise.

Generally the decision to make to customers' order comes about where demand is uncertain, where the cost of stock-building is very high or where a standard product is inappropriate. Sometimes, of course, there is no option – as for instance in the case of a garage workshop – but where there is a choice it is important that a clear-cut policy is established. Firms that try to do a bit of both finish up doing nothing at all.

There is, however, an important intermediate policy which can help to overcome some of the problems of going to one extreme or another. This is where a firm makes components to stock, only carrying out the final assembly when the orders have been received.

Which formula to use?

Two issues are involved in setting policy to answer this question, a formula being a recipe or specification for an article. The first ties in with marketing policy very closely and relates to the decisions on the quality of the product and its price. If it is a high-quality product or service and carries a high price tag, then the formula will be relatively high quality too. The second issue is that the firm may choose to allow the customer some freedom in this area and may either have a policy of building what the customer wants or simply offering products of one's own design or to a home-grown recipe. Clearly if the firm is making standard products or services, then it cannot also make products to the customers' own design and specification. If, however, the business is a jobbing shop then what the customers want can be provided.

Make by hand or by machine?

The bread-making illustration at the start of this chapter required a simple decision as regards making dough, namely whether to knead it by hand or use a machine. The machine is quicker and makes the effort of bread-making less onerous. On the other hand, equipment is expensive to buy and there is something very satisfying about kneading dough by hand. In organisations of all kinds, the question crops up frequently, Do we use people or machines? And also (at a different stage), Do we replace people with machines?

In management language the policy decision is, What is the degree of mechanisation we should try to achieve? Another way of putting it is whether the business wants to be labour intensive or capital intensive – men or machines. The answer is difficult because there are so many elements in the equation. Here are a few of the factors to take into account.

A business that is highly mechanised avoids problems of finding and keeping large numbers of people. It avoids rising labour costs and the risks of not being able to satisfy customers because of strikes or other industrial action such as working to rule. Mechanisation speeds up the productive process, raises productivity, cuts costs and eliminates many dangerous, dirty and exhausting tasks. The robots used by motorcar manufacturers are doing all these things.

On the other side of the coin, mechanisation is very expensive to install, it requires very skilled people to operate it, it is not as flexible as a human being, it can lead to a lot of people being out of work (at least in the short run), and to make money there has to be a big enough demand for the product that the equipment is kept going for most of the time. A computer that is only used six hours a day for a five-day week is not being used for a quarter of the time it should be used.

Which machine to choose and use?

The policy decisions under this question centre on the question of the type of technology to be employed. It may be just a question of choosing a particular manufacturer's products, or it may be more fundamental; for example, where heating is important, should the fuel system be gas, electricity, coal or oil?

Within this area there is also the problem of whether to buy, rent or hire equipment; basic ground rules must be established for this. So too there must be a clear-cut policy about maintenance of equipment. This usually revolves around the question, How much regular maintenance should be carried out with a view to preventing costly machine breakdowns? One extreme answer would be simply to wait until the equipment actually seized up, then fix it. Another extreme would be to have a huge team of maintenance men continually fine-tuning the equipment so that it never, ever, broke down (a solution both very costly and probably impossible).

Finally as regards equipment and machinery there is the important decision as to how fast it should be replaced. Do you run it until it collapses in bits on the floor or do you deliberately buy new every two or three years, or whenever the latest model appears?

The final set of policies that have to be established in operations are those that revolve around the purchase of the components and materials needed to make the products and help provide the services. These policy decisions are broadly similar to those which are required if the organisation was in the 'buy' not 'make' category and can therefore be considered at the same time.

Policies in buying

If you drive a car you have to put petrol in it from time to time. One of the motorist's nightmares is being stranded on a lonely road, in the middle of the night, miles from anywhere and out of petrol. To avoid the problem there are several alternative policies that could be adopted, including:

- Carry a gallon can of petrol in the boot.
- Fill up the tank every 100 miles (or some other regular interval).
- Study the price of petrol in the garages on the way out, so that you know which is cheapest on the way back.

- Calculate before you start how far you intend to travel, work out how many gallons you need, add ten per cent for emergencies and fill up accordingly.
- Having arrived at the second garage and found it more expensive, you should not take a chance, but fill up, pay up and smile.

There are a few more, but they all have one characteristic in common, namely they all indicate the need to think ahead.

It is not too critical if a car runs out of petrol, but imagine what would happen if a plane or ship ran out of fuel ten miles from home. That kind of situation cannot be allowed to happen. Similarly organisations that try to take chances as far as buying is concerned may be lucky and scrape home but often they find themselves paying a heavy price to get there. Naturally the aim is to buy as cheaply as possible. The skill of the buyer includes achieving this aim without having to live in fear that the wheels will stop turning because he has not bought enough.

The five ideas listed above for avoiding trouble are different ways of buying petrol. If we decide that we will always fill the tank up after 100 miles of travelling – irrespective of the price – we have, in effect, chosen a particular policy for buying petrol; we have a rule.

Since all organisations have to make purchases of one kind or another, even if it is only on paper, someone has to be responsible for the activity simply because of the huge sums of money that can be involved. A small shop can find itself buying goods and services worth over £100,000 a year these days.

In firms where a high proportion of total cost is materials, components and other bought out services, inefficient buying can wipe out the firm's profits entirely; all it needs is a one or two percent increase in costs.

This can be seen in a firm like Marks & Spencer, where goods are bought for resale. The importance of the buyer is not in doubt: to get the right products in the right place at the right time and with the right quality; these are the essential aims of the buyer. What then are the key issues that buyers have to deal with and for which policies can be established? There are four main ones.

Choosing suppliers

In selecting a suitable policy regarding suppliers, two basic issues have to be resolved. The first is, How many suppliers should we have? And the second is, How do we choose which organisations will supply us?

One supplier or more? The advantages of the single supplier are:

- often gives a better service (delivery, goods on credit, etc.);
- gives a better price;
- helps to establish a relationship and is therefore more likely to respond in a crisis;
- there may be economies in repair and servicing if the product is of a durable nature.

For instance, to have a fleet of aircraft consisting of just one type (say twenty Boeing 737s) is considerably less costly, in terms of holding spares and parts and in having a skilled maintenance department, than if the twenty planes consisted of six different types from four different manufacturers.

The advantages of having several suppliers are:

- safety – if one firm goes broke or on strike, delivery is still assured. Flexibility is added;

- one supplier may not be able to supply all the different types needed;
- a single supplier may become wholly dependent on your organisation if the quantities involved are particularly large. It may be advisable to 'spread the favours';
- can often obtain very good buys by only taking up 'special offers'. This is similar to the shopper who looks in all the shops each week and decides where to buy the groceries on the basis of the best discounts going at the time.

How to choose your supplier(s)

The main factors affecting choice of supplier are:

- his price;
- his ability to deliver the goods on time;
- his 'after-sales service';
- the extent of his technical support services;
- the amount of credit he gives (how long is it before he wants to be paid);
- the quality of the goods;
- any exchange arrangements (will he buy from you?);
- the supplier's financial 'health';
- his ability to meet urgent orders;
- friendship (this can override quite a few of the others).

Buying to stock or not

Everything used regularly can be bought just before it is needed. This is known as 'hand-to-mouth' buying. Or it can be bought in bulk and stored, i.e. buying 'to stock', and it is possible to buy three months', six months' or a year's consumption in one big purchase.

For example, the advantages and disadvantages of buying a year's supply of cheese (or butter or bananas) at one time are:

Bulk Buying of Fresh Foods

Main advantages

- Cheaper to obtain (bulk discount).
- Protected against a shortage of supply due to labour problems, weather, war, etc. In a factory this would ensure that production would not be held up.
- The cost will be much higher by the end of the period (this assumes inflation will happen).
- Ensures that a sudden big increase in demand can be met.

Main disadvantages

- It costs money to store the goods.
- It means spending a lot of money a long time before any comes in (it may mean borrowing too).
- The goods may go bad.
- The goods may 'shrink', which is a polite way of saying that they get pinched.
- The goods may become unpopular and only saleable as waste.

It appears therefore that the disadvantages outweigh the advantages of bulk buying at least as far as fresh food is concerned. With other products the opposite may be the case. The buyer of wine for a big hotel or off-licence group has to buy some wine in bulk many years before it is fully mature. He has to bear all the disadvantages just mentioned, because in the end the wine can sell at considerably higher prices and moreover is then unobtainable on the open market.

Even if the only goods supplied to an organisation are paper and other stationery items, a policy decision has to be made – do we buy when we need it, or carry stocks in anticipation of demand for it?

If the answer is to buy to stock, a further important rule has to be established, namely:

How much stock to carry?

The easy answer to this question is 'just enough to make sure that we can always satisfy the customers' requirements instantly'. The only problem is that to be absolutely 100 per cent sure of doing this the quantity and range of stock that would be needed to be carried would be too expensive in relation to the likely overall demand. A simple example of this is in a shoe shop. Each men's shoe can be in, say, ten different sizes with five widths for each size. That makes fifty different sized shoes for one style. If only twenty styles are carried there are one thousand different boxes of men's shoes. Even then at least two pairs of each have to be carried – probably five or six for the most popular fittings, giving a grand total of four or five thousand pairs of shoes. Even then there is a possibility a customer could come in just after the last pair had been sold. It would not make economic sense to carry so much stock.

The policy decision to be made is the level of customer satisfaction to be aimed at (whether the customer is a person who comes in and buys or is a department being supplied within the same organis-ation). A ten-per-cent satisfaction indicates that most of the time stocks are very low, which may not be a bad thing if everything is built to suit the customers' own requirements. But to try to satisfy most of the people most of the time (say eighty per cent) tells the buyer to go out and spend a lot of money.

An associated policy decision is called the 'economic

order quantity' or 'EOQ'. Properly decided and applied, the EOQ avoids embarrassing shortages on the one hand and a squirrel-like hoarding on the other.

Centralised storage or not?

The final major policy to be settled regarding buying is, Where do we store the materials (or goods) when they have been delivered?

With a single unit operation like an independent shop or a small workshop, there is no problem; the goods flow in at the back door and into a storage area. If there is more than one operation, however, there is a choice between a central store for all units or smaller stores attached to each of the operating areas. The choice for a two unit operation looks like this, in diagrammatic form (assuming similar products or services in both areas):

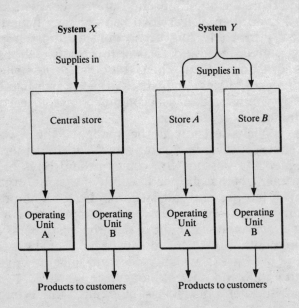

The choice will depend on such things as the distance between the two operating areas, the amount of storage space alongside each operating area and the cost of carrying a full range of stores at each location.

If the two operating units were 1,000 miles apart, it would be better to have separate storage facilities in each place, unless some other factor makes this impossible. So system Y is normally preferred here.

In contrast, if there is no convenient storage place nearby, system X has to be employed: there is no choice.

Finally, if the materials being stored are cheap it may be no problem to store them at both locations (System Y). If, however, the item to be stored is expensive – say spare jumbo-jet engines – of which no airline can afford to keep spares at every airport, the cost is prohibitive and so a central store is used.

A last word on buying policies

The benefits of having policies spelt out are considerable, and good buyers are worth their weight in gold.

9 Policies in Personnel and Industrial Relations

All companies depend for their success on people or, in management jargon, the human resource. Well-founded policies in these areas will carry a beneficial impact for management, since less time will need to be spent sorting out 'People problems' and more to developing both the business and the people within it.

One of the most effective ways of finding out about human resource management is to build a house or an extension on an existing house. There are three ways of going about the task: either you employ a reputable firm of builders who will see to everything on your behalf, or you do everything yourself from plumbing to bricklaying to the wiring. The first of these is expensive, the second is considerably cheaper but you need to be very practical and have far more spare time than most people care to give to such activities. The third alternative is to hire all the skills you need, when you need them, for as long as you need them only. It is a half-way position: you save money and save time, at least in theory.

The first of the three approaches requires some human resource management skill and the second only a little. But the third alternative contains many of the personnel and industrial relations issues that will also be found in the biggest firms. In the first place there are the purely organisational matters that come up when these questions are asked: What are the different tasks that need to be carried out to make sure that the job gets done properly? And, In which order do we want the tasks carried out? Once these have been answered, it is necessary to get answers to a range of other questions all of which fall into the category of policy issues.

Possible policy questions would include:

- What sort of people are we going to hire?
- Where do we get them?
- How much are we going to pay them?
- Are we going to offer them any other compensation?
- Are we going to bother if they are trade union members or not?
- For how long do we employ them?

It is of course perfectly possible to operate on a purely arbitrary basis, deciding the answer to each of the questions as and when needed. But this can lead to some odd discrepancies in the treatment of employees, so that some may get free overalls for instance and others do not. If significant, these discrepancies can lead to trouble – a situation which is hardly uncommon in the post-war British industrial relations scene. Indeed there is a good deal of evidence to suggest that those organisations that have had well-developed personnel and industrial relations policies for many years are the firms that have least trouble and the greatest success. No policy is bad policy.

The areas of personnel and industrial relations which need clear policies can be classified into four, namely:

- *recruitment and selection*
- *pay and conditions*
- *training and development*
- *industrial relations*

and within each area several aspects need a policy decision.

Recruitment and selection

If you decided to build a house for yourself and hire your own labour, you could proceed in several ways. You could:

- Place a large sign in front of the site saying, 'Men wanted for building work. Apply within'.
- Ask your friends for names of reliable individuals with special skills (carpentry, bricklaying etc.).
- Ask someone in the trade (e.g. a carpenter) for names.
- Look for these skills being advertised in the local paper.
- Advertise in the local paper.

Some of these are clearly better than others – simply to advertise for 'men' would be to invite trouble on two counts. First, the Sex Discrimination Act of 1975 forbids that kind of advertising. Most jobs must be open to both men and women. Second, to advertise for people without specifying what type of skills and experience are needed attracts large numbers of people who are quite unsuitable for the jobs needed. The first possibility is therefore out. The second and third possibilities are common for small jobbing work: to have someone working for you who has been recommended is reassuring and often a good arrangement. The fourth and fifth choices are also possibles, but require a careful screening process to ensure that the people taken on are competent to do the job.

This illustrates the point that recruitment of staff centres upon three questions:

- What sort of people do we need?
- How are we going to get them?
- Where do we get them from?

What kind of people do we need?

This question is not as simple as it appears at first glance. Obviously an organisation that does no planning at all is asking the question daily, as work fails to get done on time, if at all. Most organisations, however, try to establish well in advance what their staffing requirements will be. This activity is known as 'personnel planning' – a highly complex, and necessary, function.

The personnel planning operation has to work within the broad strategic framework of the organisation and in accordance with the policy decisions made in the various functional areas such as sales and production. These factors determine both the types and quantities of staff needed at specified dates in the future, the need arising partly because staff will have to be replaced from time to time (as they retire or get promoted or leave), and partly because of changes in the strategies of the organisation.

The policy decisions which will help to make the personnel planner's life easier are four in number. First, the kind of age profile the organisation wants. It should be kept in mind, however, that organisations may want a corporate age profile that is unusual for many reasons. For instance, one company may not want to hire people over the age of thirty, whereas another may never recruit anyone under that age.

The second policy decision in this area is concerned with qualifications. Again there is a choice. Some organisations may be prepared to take on anyone who has the ability and experience to do the job; others will insist on certain minimum qualifications as well. For example many large companies insist that promotion to a managerial grade is only possible if that person has a university degree. Another example is the organisation that insists that all its accounts department staff should be members of the Institute of Chartered Accountants, not hiring staff who are members of other similar institutions.

The third area where a policy decision needs taking is that related to experience, some preferring no experience of the work so that training can be related to the precise requirements of the organisation, others looking for experienced people who can adapt.

Finally, there is the question of hiring people who have potential for higher posts within the organisation. Some firms recruit people in relation to the specific job that is vacant without regard to any future requirements. Other firms try to employ people who seem capable of taking on greater responsibilities after a few years' experience.

How are we going to get them?

The policy choice which is built in to this question is, Do we recruit the people we need, when we need them, or do we try to develop our own staff in anticipation of need?

The first course of action (a hand-to-mouth policy) has the advantage that there is more chance of getting a better-qualified person than if the only people available were home-grown. Moreover there is some argument for bringing in new people from outside in that new blood is good for the body. The disadvantages are that often it is more expensive to obtain new staff than to promote existing personnel, and there is a risk that the new staff member may not in the end be suitable for the job. A sensible policy regarding recruitment of new staff is clearly needed and this should minimise the chances of getting a dud, but even so the risk is there.

In contrast, the advantages of the planned development policy are, first, that it is cheaper; second, it increases the chances of getting the right type of person for the job and, third, the person appointed can be effective more quickly in the new post because there is little or no settling-in time. Finally, the prospects of promotion from within, if strong, may well provide a motive for better work.

The disadvantages of growing one's own talent are, first, that the talent may leave the organisation after being trained; second, an organisation that tries never to recruit from outside (especially at the managerial level) runs the risk of producing an inward-looking top management team, short of ideas.

Where do we get them from?

The main policy decisions that need to be taken in this respect are whether recruitment is to be open to all, or limited in some special way by, for example, only advertising in local newspapers or only in the *Sunday Times*. A further decision is whether to recruit directly oneself or use the services of an agency.

Organisations often have to develop policies about all kinds of selection matters, such as racial or sex discrimination; health; working for a competitor, and even religion.

Finally there is the question of getting rid of staff. All organisations must have clearly set out rules for dismissal and redundancy. It must be made known to every employee under what conditions they could be dismissed, and a policy established for dealing with staff who are surplus to requirements – either because of a trade recession or because the nature of the business has changed. It is also worth deciding in advance if the policy on redundancy is 'first in, first out' or 'last in, first out'.

Pay and conditions

'Pay and conditions' is a shorthand phrase for all the benefits an employer brings (or could bring) to an employee, ranging in importance from basic wages and salaries through bonus systems and hours of work to such intangibles as the physical conditions of the place of work. There are several important policy matters relating to this aspect of personnel management, as follows:

General levels of pay

While many organisations (but not in the public sector) try to have general pay levels roughly similar to 'the going rate' to be found around and about, many firms have a policy of deliberately paying higher (or lower) rates of pay than ordinarily found. The high-rate-of-pay policy is to be found in the organisation that believes it is only by paying high wages and salaries it is getting the best people. The economic justification is that the 'best people' will actually make the firm much more profitable, thus more than paying for their high cost. While this may be true in some cases, there is also some evidence to suggest that a very high level of salaries and wages is no guarantee of much improved perform-ance in a firm. It does seem, however, that a higher than average level of pay can lead to a reduced level of industrial action, such as less strike action.

In contrast a low-rate-of-pay policy is one where the firm has decided to take a fairly tough attitude towards pay increases and works hard to keep general awards in line with the minimum to be found (such as the trade union's minimum wage). The economic justification for this policy is that by keeping total wage costs low, general price increases can be kept low too. Thus demand for the company's products or services will remain high, ensuring work for all employees in the firm.

Internal pay consistency

Imagine what would happen if whenever someone was hired in a large company like ICI or Shell the persons making the appointment were able to fix the pay of the newcomer. Within a very short time there would be a great deal of trouble. Similarly, imagine what would happen if you were working in a firm and the boss called you into his office and told you he was giving you an immediate rise of £20,000 a year, and then a few days later you discovered that all your colleagues had been given increases of £22,000 a year. How would you feel? What would you do?

A debate which often comes up in this connection is concerned with geographic differences. For example two secretaries work in the same firm, doing identical jobs. One works in London, the other in Leeds. Should there be any pay differential? Many organisations, both public and private, recognise the need to adjust pay if the cost of living is higher in one part of the country than in another. In Britain the 'London allowance' is quite common, and organisations like the United Nations have very complicated allowances adjusting pay from country to country depending on relative living costs.

Merit awards

It has been recognised for a long time that some individuals work harder and with a higher quality of results than others. It is a matter of policy if, and how far, this should be recognised and rewarded. It is not difficult to establish relative efficiency where individuals' work can be measured precisely, such as for salesmen. There it is normal to give the salesman a small percentage of the value of every order over a certain minimum quantity. In the same way in factories if output exceeds a certain basic level those achieving the excess share a bonus.

The problem is more difficult in offices and in other situations where it is difficult to identify diligence and superior work. Many public service organisations have no merit award system for this reason, arguing that it is the diligent and 'better' employee who gets promoted.

Profit-sharing schemes

A popular form of bonus is to give all employees a share in the profits of the firm. This may be a fixed percentage of the profits of the firm, so that if the firm had a bad year no bonus would be given, but in a boom time, the bonus could be high.

While everyone likes a 'free gift' of money, objections to such a policy are that it cannot be fair. If the sum is distributed on the basis of basic pay (e.g. five per cent of pay) or if it is a flat sum (e.g. £500 per head) someone is bound to complain. Someone else would complain if it was given 'on merit'. Profit sharing is not uncommon, but needs careful handling.

Fringe benefits

It is a matter of policy whether an organisation gives its employees any other benefits besides basic pay. Such benefits include cars, pension funds, free or cut-price meals, interest-free loans, long holidays and shorter working hours.

Some of these are taken for granted, like holidays and pension funds. Some organisations add on many items in an attempt to get hold of the right kind of staff. How many fringe benefits, and how far to go, are important decisions and will be based partly on the following considerations:

- Is it normal for the type of business?
- Can I get the staff only by offering such attractions?
- Is the profit of the business likely to be higher if I give out many benefits?
- Who in the company will enjoy the benefits and who will be left out? And what do I tell the ones who are left out?

Other conditions

While minimum health and safety standards are set out by law for people at work, through such legislation as the Health and Safety at Work Act 1974, there can be a world of difference in the standards of the working environment in one organisation as compared with another – not only in connection with health and safety matters but in such things as the location of the organisation, the standard of décor, furniture and fittings. As always there are merits and demerits of a policy to ignore or foster considerations such as these. Often the decision hangs on whether the top management in the organisation believes these elements to be of importance in recruiting, keeping and motivating staff.

Training and development

From the discussion earlier in this chapter it will be obvious that training depends largely on various other policies in the personnel area. If an organisation intends to hire people simply for the immediate job that needs to be done, then any training is optional. In contrast, firms that recruit in anticipation of need, or that have a policy of growing their own talent, will by definition have to get involved in training to a much greater extent.

Several different types of training can be identified in all organisations. These are:

- Training for the immediate job to be done; for instance, helping a new sales assistant in a shop learn how to deal with customers.
- Training in understanding the immediate environment of the employee; for instance, giving that sales assistant the opportunity to learn more about the company and how it operates.
- Training to prepare for promotion. The sales assistant attending training programmes for sales supervisors would be a common example of this. A more sophisticated way of handling this would be to expose the assistant to some of the supervisor's normal work load and get them to do it. This is sometimes known as 'action learning'.
- Training for general all-round improved efficiency and understanding. This could be where the same sales assistant is given the chance to learn more about business generally, or to keep up to date, or to acquire new skills – for instance in computer programming.

In all these situations, the organisation has to determine the extent to which it is going to encourage staff at all levels to develop. This to some extent depends on the future needs of the organisation and also on how rapidly the environment is changing. A company at the forefront of technology, in information processing for example, may find its staff being called upon to possess new skills and knowledge quite suddenly. This could be fatal if that firm had not been developing its key staff in anticipation.

Not only is the problem one of extent, but the other key issues are, To what extent are we going to train our people inside the organisation? Are we going to rely on external agencies to train for us? And, How much time and money should we give staff who want to go away and train themselves?

Training and development of managers

Particular emphasis needs to be placed on the training and development of managers. It is, of course, entirely up to the organisation how much time and money it puts into managerial development, but there are very few sound arguments against doing no training. On the other hand there are a number of very good reasons for putting considerable effort into the activity.

The arguments against include:

- It costs too much.
- Once trained they will leave.
- Once trained they will be discontented.
- Once trained too many questions will be asked.

The arguments for are:

- The increasing complexity of organisations requires that managers have to be knowledgeable about more and more things to be effective.
- Managers have to understand, or have a thorough working knowledge of, all aspects of the part of the organisation for which they are responsible. Top managers by definition need to know about all aspects of their organisation.
- Without adequate preparation for higher levels of responsibility, a manager can be promoted beyond his level of competence (this is known as the 'Peter Principle').
- Only if a manager has some understanding of other parts of the organisation will he be able to communicate with them (and they with him!) and gain their trust and goodwill.

■ The environment is changing so fast that it is not reasonable to expect the manager to keep up to date in all the things he should be up to date on: an out-of-date manager being a dangerous animal.

Industrial relations

When anyone starts working for an organisation it is normal to establish precisely what pay and conditions will be given to that person in exchange for his time, skills and effort. It is, in effect, a contract between an employer and an employee and is reviewed and renewed at least once a year. In very small organisations the process can be carried out on an informal basis between individuals and senior management; each person effectively doing his own bargaining and negotiating.

As organisations grow, however, individual bargaining becomes impracticable and so systems are developed for classifying groups of employees into categories for pay and conditions purposes. Changes in the levels of pay within categories or grades are handled by representatives drawn from employees or by representatives of a trade union. In essence, therefore, industrial relations policy matters are concerned with the relationships between the organisation and trade unions or other staff representatives.

The choices that exist for management can best be seen by looking at a number of specific questions which have to be answered if sound rules for negotiations are wanted:

To what extent do we want our staff to have their pay and conditions negotiated by trade unions?

Often this question is irrelevant because it is traditional in many sectors of the economy for unions to carry out negotiations. Where this is not the case, a choice exists and the answer will depend on the efficiency of existing negotiating systems, on the track record of the unions involved, on the wishes of the staff themselves and on the attitude of the decision-makers towards trade unions in general.

What should our attitude be towards the unions?

A whole range of possible answers can be given to this question. At one extreme there is the 'necessary evil' attitude, which results in considerable effort being spent in trying to frustrate the work of the union in such matters as the disclosure of information to staff on company performance or plans ('Don't tell them anything') or deliberately putting off decisions about fringe benefits.

At the other extreme there is the cooperative approach which views the role of the unions as essential for the future wellbeing of the business. In this situation full consultation takes place on all matters, small requests are handled quickly and information is offered freely before it is requested.

There are many shades of attitude between these two extremes and it has to be remembered in choosing a particular policy that it is often very difficult to move from a 'hard' position to a more cooperative relationship. This is because attitudes may be so well dug in on either side of the relationship that change is almost impossible.

How far should we involve the unions?

This question clearly stems from the last one. Again, the extremes can fairly easily be identified: there is the 'pay and hours only' school of thought which is the traditional view of collective bargaining, representing one extreme. At the other end there is the view that there ought to be some employee representation on the highest decision-making bodies in the organisation. In other words, employees should have a say in the future shape of the business. This idea is found in practice in Germany, but has been seriously considered in Britain only since 1977, when the Bullock Report* was published. Although the committee's conclusions were attacked in many quarters, the contents make interesting reading on the merits and demerits of employee representatives taking a seat in the boardroom.

In the event of a dispute how far should the organisation try to avoid damaging industrial action?

Even in the best-run organisations (from an industrial relations point of view) serious differences arise from time to time between the claims of the employees and what the management side of the negotiating table considers appropriate. For instance if the union asks for a thirty-five-per-cent increase in basic pay and the company considers that only five per cent is justified, a situation is in the making that could lead to trouble. Some organisations adopt a policy of giving the union as much as possible, irrespective of the cost, an 'anything for a quiet life' policy. Other organisations, at the other extreme, try never to compromise but are actually prepared to tolerate strike action, rather than appear to be giving in. Again the extent to which an organisation veers to one or the other extreme depends

* *Report of Committee of Inquiry on Industrial Democracy* (HMSO, 1977).

on the nature of the business, but more importantly on the attitudes of the participants in the bargaining process.

Finally on industrial relations policies, a quotation from *The Bullock Report* is worthy of consideration:

> There must in the future be a new legitimacy for the exercise of the management function within a policy framework agreed jointly by the representatives of capital and labour. We believe that this legitimacy is essential for the long-term efficiency and profitability of the private sector and for the ultimate success of the economy itself.
>
> We do not think that this will be achieved unless employee representatives are fully involved in, and committed to the work of, the board, and share equally with the shareholder representatives the responsibility for the board's decisions. In our view it is unreasonable to expect employee representatives to accept equal responsibility, unless, through equal representation on the board, they are able to have equal influence on the decision-making process.

10 Financial Policies

Business aims and objectives are more often than not of a financial nature. Business enterprises are there to 'make money'. Policy decisions in the way money is handled are, therefore, of prime importance in business.

Most people, as individuals, have dealings with money. Even school children receiving pocket money each week have to learn to handle it and soon realise that because there is a limited amount of it, care has to be taken with what they do with it. As adults, the quantity of money passing through our hands is usually a lot more than a schoolboy's pocket money; unfortunately adult needs for money are greater than the schoolboy's. The problem is that the quantity of money coming in rarely seems enough for all the needs we have, needs that only money can satisfy. Occasionally more money comes in than we need and when that situation occurs we have the different problem of deciding what to do with it.

All organisations are faced with exactly the same problem, the main difference being the sheer size of the numbers involved. Whereas the average British wage-earner will bring home several thousands of pounds in a year (say, £5,000) the biggest British companies pull in from sales hundreds of millions of pounds in a year (say, £2,000,000,000).

There is, however, another difference that exists between individuals and commercial organisations. This is that commercial organisations usually have to spend money before it comes in from trading. For instance the baker has to buy his ovens and premises, his flour, yeast and salt. He has to buy all of these things before he can sell his bread. Until he sells the product no money can come in.* Unfortunately he has to spend before he can receive money, but there is no guarantee that he will sell anything at all; he could make 1,000 loaves of bread only to find that the weather takes a turn for the worse, storms and gales keep people indoors and no bread gets sold. The bread goes stale, it is thrown away and the baker has lost money.

The wage– or salary-earner in contrast does at least know that his pay will arrive at the end of each week or month and he does know approximately how much he will receive. The butcher, the baker and all have no such guarantee. They have to set themselves up to trade at their own expense. They are risking their own money and that of their fellow shareholders.

Policies regarding money, usually known as 'financial policies', therefore, revolve around two basic questions:

- From where do we get money?
- How should it be used?

In financial language these two questions are referred to as dealing with the sources of finance (or funds) and the uses of finance (or funds).

* It must be remembered too that the amount of money actually in an organisation is not the same thing as profit. Profit can be defined as the difference between what is sold and the cost of making the sale. If the baker sells a loaf for 30p and the ingredients cost 20p then his profit is 10p on a loaf. By selling 1,000 loaves he would make a profit of £100 out of which he has to pay all the wages and the other overheads of the business. Then he can calculate his profit. But as to how much money he has – it could be anything. All the bread might have been sold on credit, the baker would have bought next week's flour and put it into the storeroom – that particular transaction does not get included in the profit calculation until it is turned into bread and sold.

Sources of finance

There are four main sources of finance for any company. It may come from the owners of the business (the shareholders); from lenders such as banks; from a sale of part of the business; or from the firm's own trading activities. Each source has its own merits and demerits, and if a firm wants to raise money it may be guided by pre-established policies. The main factors influencing the choice for each are considered in the following pages.

Finance from the owners

All business operations begin with finance supplied by the owners. As we saw in Chapter 2, this is usually called the share capital of the business and this simply means that anyone who buys a share in a company becomes a part owner.

If a company wants to inject more share capital into the firm it would have to:

- make sure it could legally sell more shares;
- offer the extra shares at a specified price on the market. This is usually done by inviting existing shareholders to buy extra shares at a favourable price. This is known as a 'rights issue', and is offered to shareholders in direct proportion to the number of shares they already hold;
- be fairly sure that the existing shareholders will be willing to take up their rights. (In other words the dividend and growth record has to be attractive).

So long as these three conditions are fulfilled, a policy of raising money via rights issues is relatively simple and inexpensive.

An alternative way of raising new finance in the form

of share capital is to offer additional shares on the open market. This policy, usually these days referred to as an 'offer for sale', is used when large sums of money are involved or where, for some reason, it is felt that a rights issue might not succeed. It can also be used in the process of turning a privately owned company into a public company.

The policy decision to raise more share capital depends partly on the overall financial structure of the business (which will be examined later), partly on the sum of money required, partly on the acceptability of the company as a good risk (i.e. the chances of losing your money are not too high), partly on its prospects and partly on whether the present owners are prepared to lose some of their control of the business (in terms of ownership).

Finance from lenders

The policy issue in raising money by way of borrowing can be summarised in the following question: How much should we borrow?

From time to time every organisation finds that it needs to borrow some money. The need may be temporary, such as when a farmer has to buy the fertilizer and seed early in the year, or it may be on a much longer-term basis, such as when an airline borrows to buy new planes, paying back the borrowing over several years. These two different types of borrowing are usually referred to as short-term borrowing or 'current liabilities', and long-term or 'loan' capital. The total amount borrowed is sometimes referred to by the American term 'debt'.

Short-term borrowing. There are two kinds of short-term borrowing. One is where the organisation does not pay its bills (having actually received the goods or service;

and may include a tax bill too!), the other is where money is actually borrowed to pay the bills or the wages or the taxman.

Some organisations have a rule that no money should be owed for more than a few days and that borrowing on a short-term basis should be avoided if at all possible. The main reason given is that short-term borrowing is very expensive in terms of the high interest charges that have to be paid on the amount of money borrowed. In addition, paying your bills very quickly can sometimes save money. Some suppliers allow 'prompt payment' discounts, so that if the bill is paid up within seven days a small percentage can be taken off the total owed.

To be able to pay all the bills on time and avoid having to borrow from the bank requires the organisation to be fairly sure of receiving money in through sales. In addition it has to have well-developed cash forecasting systems to make sure the money paid out never exceeds the amount flowing in.

At the other end of the scale there are many organisations that put off paying their bills as long as they possibly can and do not seem to mind how high their overdraft is at the bank. There are, however, limits to all this borrowing. Banks do have rules to prevent overdrafts getting too high and suppliers can stop supplying if their bills are not paid. The limit depends on the amount of money flowing in and how trustworthy and stable the organisation is (known usually as credit-worthiness). Within these limits, however, it is a key organisational policy decision how much short-term borrowing to undertake.

Long-term borrowing. Organisations borrow money on a long-term basis when they want to grow but either do not have sufficient of their own, or cannot raise more from shareholders. Some companies have a policy of never raising finance in this way, preferring to plough back the profits of the business. The big advantage of borrowing is that it enables the firm to grow faster than if it relied on its own, and the shareholders', funds. This is not to assert that fast growth is automatically desirable, but it is sometimes necessary if, for instance, a competitor is planning to attack one of the firm's best markets; there has to be a quick response to the threat, and borrowing enables the firm to meet that threat faster.

Another advantage of long-term borrowing is that it should increase the amount of money available to each shareholder. This can be better appreciated if we look at the case of Len's Launderette.

Len owned a very busy, old-established launderette which produced for him a profit last year of £8,000 after tax had been paid. Normally Len took most of this profit out of the business, so that the equity capital of the firm hardly rose year after year.

One day Len was offered another launderette on a prime site for £40,000. On its own this business could bring in £8,000 as well, but by combining the two shops together the total profit could be as much as £20,000 after tax, because of the effect of synergy (see page 96). Len could not afford to buy this second launderette himself, although he really would have liked to. He spoke to his brother-in-law, who immediately replied that he would gladly find £40,000 and put it into the business, in exchange for half of all the profits.

Len thought about this for a long time. Half the profits of the total business was £10,000: quite a bit more than his present earnings; it sounded an attractive proposition. However he decided to have a chat with the bank manager whom he had known for a long time. The bank manager heard Len's story, then gave his opinion that a loan would probably be available to Len if he wanted it.

'What about the interest?' asked Len. To which the bank manager replied that even if it was at fifteen per cent a year Len would still be better off because he would not have to share the profits. He then proceeded to prove his point with some simple figures:

First situation: using brother-in-law's money

Trading profit before tax:	£33,300
Less: Tax at 40% (approx.):	−£13,300
Profit after tax:	£20,000
B-in-law's share (i.e. half):	−£10,000
Left for Len:	£10,000

Second situation: using borrowed money

Trading profit:	£33,300	
Less: Interest on £40,000 at 15%:	−£6,000	
Profit before tax:	£27,300	
Less: Tax at 40% (approx.):	−£10,900	
Profit after tax:	−£16,400	All for Len!

The bank manager went on to explain about the type of loan that could be made, the security for the loan, some other tax angles and how the loan repayments could be made. In the end, Len agreed that it sounded the best possible alternative – but he said, 'the trouble is, it sounds a bit risky to me'.

Financial risk

The risk, and this applies to *all* borrowing, is that there is no guarantee that trading profits will turn out as high as planned. What *is* certain is that the interest payments will have to be made and if trading profits fell enough, Len could end up worse off. Even more difficult would be the situation that trading profits turned out to be less than the interest due.

All organisations that choose to borrow face a similar

risk. The decision that has to be taken at the policy level is: at what level of borrowing does the risk become acceptable? To put it another way, if we borrow more, what are the chances of our trading performance deteriorating (because of intense competition, recessions, strikes, changes in fashion, etc.) to such an extent that we cannot pay out any dividend to shareholders or, even worse, be unable to pay the interest?

Finally, in respect of long-term loans, it should be noted that once the major policy decision is taken regarding the extent of such borrowing, further policy decisions have to be taken regarding the precise type of borrowing. There are many different types of loan: preference shares, debentures, mortgages, secured and unsecured loans, medium-term to long-term, fixed or variable interest rates, loans raised at home or abroad, and so on. All have to be discussed, analysed and ranked in terms of which are most suitable for the company. Needless to say each type has its merits and drawbacks, but that is beyond the scope of this book.

Finance from selling off part of the business

There are two aspects to this method of raising money, and neither actually produces new additional capital, merely converts existing assets into cash. First there is the 'sale and leaseback' arrangement where an organisation that owns some land or a building sells that asset to (usually) an insurance company or pension fund. At the same time a contract is drawn up enabling the firm to lease the asset from the new owners for a fixed term of years. The seller gets the capital value of the asset and its use, in exchange for what amounts, in effect, to a long-term rental agreement.

A policy to engage in this kind of activity to any extent must naturally correlate with the basic 'rent not buy' policy of the business. This type of policy, where the company chooses to lease or rent as much of its fixed assets as possible, has the advantage of not requiring so much capital, but it does naturally result in lower profits because of the rental or leasing costs. A company that chooses a 'buy not rent' policy will not normally want to get involved in sale or leaseback activities unless it is in a 'cash flow crisis' and other sources of finance are not possible.

The second aspect to selling off part of the business is where the firm needs finance and chooses to get rid of some activity it no longer considers to be suitable. A variety of policies are found in practice, for instance:

- Hang on to it as long as it brings in a little money.
- Get rid of it if it fails to make fifteen per cent return on the capital invested in it (or some other percentage).
- Sell it while it is still a very profitable activity (i.e. before it gets old, in the case of an asset, or before the product's life-cycle stage is reached when it is on the wane), to get the best possible price.
- Get rid of it if we can find something else that will make more money.
- Sell it if it no longer fits our overall product and market strategies.

These are deceptively simple choices; in fact the mathematics involved in what has become known as the 'abandonment decision' are fairly complex. Suffice it to say that an organisation that sells off assets or activities because of financial pressure cannot succeed like the firm that has a clear policy regarding the timing of the sales.

Finance from trading activities

Most firms obtain most finance as a direct result of their trading activities. The amount that becomes available to companies is closely tied up with a specific policy decision about dividends and this is discussed first.

Dividend policy (How much should we pay the shareholders?) In Chapter 2 (page 38) we noted that profit after tax is available to the company to pay out to shareholders in the form of dividends or to put back into the business to help provide funds for tomorrow's expansion plans. The way in which the total after-tax profit is divided is up to the top management of the business – in the shape of the directors. In law they recommend to the shareholders at the annual general meeting of the company how much dividend should be paid out. The shareholders can agree or decide to reduce the dividend; they cannot vote to raise it, and usually they take the directors' advice.

It is therefore up to top management to decide how much will be given out and how much kept. The decision can be simplified by following a particular predetermined policy and there are several to choose from.

Always pay a fixed percentage of the profits. This implies that the shareholders' dividends will rise and fall as the profits of the firms rise and fall. In good times dividends are high, in bad times dividends are low. This kind of policy, sometimes referred to as the 'constant payout percentage', may be good when business is expected to do well in the foreseeable future. The disadvantage is that the shareholder never knows what dividends to expect, making his planning more difficult. The result of this kind of policy is that the shares, if quoted on a stock market, are not likely to be popular.

Always try to pay a bit more each year. The diagram over-leaf illustrates how this might work in practice. Dividends grow as profits grow but not as fast so that if profits slump there is still some margin for the shareholder.

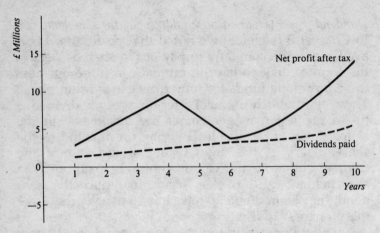

It will be noticed that the dividend line is only gradually rising when profits are forging ahead, but as profits slip so the company tries to keep the dividends at least at the level of the earlier years. It would not actually matter if profits in year six fell below the dividend line, because a company can pay dividends out of earlier years' profits if it wishes – a policy not to be pursued too often, as this is in effect reducing the size of the firm.

This type of 'stable dividend' policy is fairly popular these days in Britain, although there are a number of variations on the basic theme. Some firms will pay out a fixed proportion of the profits in dividends as long as profits are rising (usually a low proportion). If profits fall, the actual amount of dividend paid out is maintained at the previous year's level.

The advantages of the stable dividend policy are that shareholders know where they stand and are more likely to support a request for further finance. The disadvantages are that in a very good year the firm may retain more profit than it needs and in a poor year may have to dip into earlier year's profits to pay the dividend.*

Give the shareholders what's left. The third broad type of dividend policy is really a non-policy, since it has regard first to the needs of the company and only then considers the shareholder. It is sometimes referred to as the 'residual dividends policy', hence the belief that the shareholder is not the prime beneficiary in the business but the last beneficiary or the 'residual legatee'.

Money comes from being efficient

Finally as regards raising finance from operations, there is the simple but very important expedient of trying to be more efficient all round. If a company cuts its costs while maintaining standards and overall sales, then there will be more profit available for retention and future growth. Similarly selling off surplus capacity, as we have seen, generates money which can be put to better use. In the same way careful housekeeping in relation to stock levels and money outstanding from sales (i.e. debtors) can also generate money to finance growth and improved efficiency.

Overall financial structure

The various ways of raising money that we have discussed fall into two categories:

- those that increased the total size of the business

---

* It should be noted, in trying to work out what dividend policy various British firms have, that during the 1970s there were government limits on what companies could pay out as dividends. This distorts the record historically.

(i.e. raising more share capital; additional borrowing);
- those that only increased the amount of money in the business (i.e. selling off assets; reducing stock levels).

Financial structure is concerned with the first category – the question of the size of the business in money terms – and refers specifically to the different ways that a firm can raise money. It may be thought of as a wall consisting of several different types of brick:

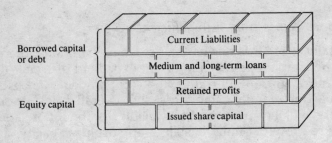

The merits and demerits of each row of bricks have already been discussed. There is, however, one main issue where a policy decision is needed and that is the question of the relative size of the 'debt' part of the structure and the relative size of the 'equity' part; in financial terms the relationship between debt and equity is called 'gearing' (in America it is known as 'leverage').*

The advantages of each type of finance have already been described, but to follow either the debt or the equity path depends first and foremost on the overall financial structure the business is prepared to accept. Briefly the alternatives are:

* There are many definitions of gearing, and many ways to measure it; take care.

- We will borrow as much as we can lay our hands on.
- We will always try to get by with as little borrowing as possible.
- Our aim is to have a gearing ratio of one to one (i.e. equal amounts of debt and equity).
- We will raise finance when we need it whichever way is cheapest.

The problem for organisations is this: in any new venture there is an ordinary commercial risk that the idea may be a failure. If the project has been financed out of borrowings then there is, in addition, a financial risk. The more a firm borrows, the higher the financial risk (but equally the greater the possible profit).

Remember Len's Launderette on pages 177–8? If Len had borrowed the money he would have been more 'highly geared' than before and he would have made much more money. But if his trading profit fell to £10,000 his results would have been:

	Using borrowed money	Using b-in-laws's money
Trading profit:	£10,000	£10,000
Less: Interest on loan at 15%	£ 6,000	—
Profit before tax:	£ 4,000	£10,000
Less: Tax at 40%	£ 1,600	£ 4,000
Profit after tax:	£ 2,400 (All for Len).	£ 6,000 (Of which £3,000 for Len).

The conclusion is that, by borrowing, Len would be better off in good times and worse off in bad times compared to his position if he had raised the money by means of extra equity capital. His decision is based on how much risk he was prepared to take and whether he wanted to keep total control of the business.

Len's Launderette, Part 2: Len decided to borrow the money to buy the second launderette, and after it had been operating for several months it was obvious that the profits would be even better than expected – thanks partly to the fact that inflation had put the charges up. So Len went to the bank manager again and asked if it would be possible to borrow another £40,000 to £50,000 for a third launderette. What do you think the bank manager said after he had seen the figures?

He would probably have advised Len to wait a couple of years, pay off some of the existing debt and plough some of the profits back to form the basis for the finance of the third launderette. Borrowing an extra £40,000–plus would put Len's gearing too high, bearing in mind the uncertainty of profits.

The example neatly leads into the other type of policy question regarding finance that was put early in the chapter (page 173) namely, How should money be used?, or 'uses of finance'.

The basic rule is that short-term finance is used for short-term needs. For instance, the bank overdraft facility is used to tide people and companies over a temporary cash shortage; it is not recommended for use in buying factories or houses.

Capital expenditure policies

As far as long-term finance is concerned (whether it is debt or equity) the rule is that it should be put to profitable use within the organisation.

This clearly depends on the overall strategies that the organisation has already chosen. However the specific uses will be determined by the different operating functions within the organisation, like operations or sales. Even so, each part of the business will come up with many proposals for spending capital on new ideas –

the problem is choosing which to adopt. To help in the decision, some basic policy decisions have to be made, setting up rules which have to be complied with in making the selection.

The underlying problem is that the higher the potential return on a venture the greater is the risk, and the lower the risk, the lower the return. To put £1,000 on a horse in the Grand National at odds of 100 to 1 is very risky, but carries a potentially very high return. To put the money in the bank at ten per cent would not give you that much return but the money would at least be safe (if an unknown bank was chosen the risk would be greater. Would you put your money in the Bank of Antarctica?).

Therefore, the decisions all organisations have to make on investing are:

- To what extent are we prepared to risk money in uncertain commercial ventures?
- What basic returns are we expecting on our investments? (Some firms state for example that 'we will invest in anything as long as it gives us a return of more than twenty per cent'.)
- To what extent do we go for a 'mixture' of investments bearing in mind that there is this relationship between risk and return?

These decisions may refer to separate activities within a total organisation or they may refer to certain characteristics of products within an operation. What is often sought is a balanced portfolio of sub-activities, or products.

One method of classifying a product portfolio has been developed by the Boston Consulting Group.*

* This concept has recently been reviewed thoroughly in the *Financial Times*. See 'Further reading'.

They have identified four basic product characteristics, like this:

		Company market share	
		High	Low
Growth rate of the product	High	1 Stars	2 Problem children
	Low	3 Cash cows	4 Dogs

'Stars' are products that are growing very fast and, because of the company's high share in the market, likely to do very well in the future. However at this stage the product is sucking money in (for development costs, extra advertising and so on). 'Cash cows' are products that have passed through the high growth stage, are now mature and no investment in them is needed. They simply 'make money'.

'Problem children' products could do well if the growth continues but the investment required is greater than for stars. There is a chance of success if it turns the low market share into a high share. There is also a chance of them turning into 'dogs'. Dogs are products to get rid of; their volume is too low to fully utilise the resources assigned to them and they are probably not contributing much by way of profit to the business. All firms need to have policies with regard to the extent that their products fall within these categories and to make sure that the product range portfolio does not get out of balance.

Policy decisions in the area of finance are clearly important. Some organisations operate on a hit-or-miss basis, simply taking financial decisions in an *ad hoc* way as and when they occur. This is neither particularly clever nor wise since the risks involved are very often too high to be left to unplanned decisions. The wise organisation – whatever its size – has financial plans carefully worked out to coincide with its strategies and aims, and has a series of rules already taken, to meet most eventualities. Many of the rules cannot be discussed here – such things as holding foreign currency, how much to carry in the bank and what to do about customers who do not pay. Nevertheless they, and the ones we have discussed, are important because the ultimate success or failure of a business (or even an organisation's ability to survive) will depend in the end on its financial strength and prospects.

11 Management Control Systems

In this chapter our concern is with the questions:

- What is control and why is it necessary?
- How can we make sure controls are effective and really work?
- What are the features of any control that make it effective?

One of the most famous sketches to appear on television or film concerns the man at the end of a conveyor belt in a large factory. His job is fairly simple, consisting of making some small adjustment to the product passing in front of him. For instance, he may be pasting a label on to a carton which has already been filled with the items made further back down the line. It is not an uncommon scene; the job is repetitive but the operator has enough time to moisten the labels, make sure each one is securely fixed to the carton and is the right way up. The sketch we see involves the gradual increase in the speed of the conveyor belt. We are never told the reason for the change in the conveyor's speed, and the operator is powerless to do anything about it. At first he does not complain, because the increase is so small that he can cope with only a little extra effort. Gradually he finds he cannot label each carton properly – some get missed completely, some have the labels on upside down or sideways; he tries to push the cartons back only to cause them to pile up on top of each other. Eventually the situation gets totally out of hand, the conveyor belt grinds to a halt with cartons all over the place and the factory looks as though a tornado has been through it.

The key phrase used to describe what happened is 'out of hand'. An equally common expression would be that the situation got out of control. Every day we come across situations that are out of control – either in our day-to-day work, or we read about them or see them happening. Typical examples are the racing car that spins off the track, the ship that runs aground, a rioting crowd or a fire that cannot be put out.

All these are highly undesirable situations, and it is probably true to state that any situation that is out of control is also undesirable, although it may not be as dramatic as those quoted above.

We describe these situations as having got out of control, or out of hand, because things were not turning out as expected or as planned: things are turning out quite different to what we expected – usually with a worse result – and we are powerless to do anything about it.

Conversely, control is making sure that any small change in the way things are working is sorted out quickly before it can do any damage. It is to stop the ship going on to the rocks, to prevent the factory from having its machinery jammed up, and to make sure that we do arrive at our destination without incurring excessive cost.

As far as the manager is concerned, it is part of his job to make sure that things do not get out of hand in the areas for which he is responsible. If he is wise he will invent (or have created for him) a method or system which will reduce the risk of things getting out of control.

The essential ingredients for the manager of our imaginary factory to give him a system of control over the flow of goods along the conveyor are:

- A standard or 'normal' speed for the conveyor.
- A device for measuring the actual speed of the conveyor.
- Something or somebody checking that the actual speed is not faster than the standard speed.
- The checking has to be done at regular intervals, e.g. every five minutes.
- A method of informing the manager if the actual speed of the conveyor exceeds the standard speed by a specified amount.
- The information has to get to the manager as fast as possible.
- An ability on the manager's part to be able to do something about the difference in speed.
- The manager must do something!

From this list it is possible to draw up a list of the elements which are needed if there is to be an effective control system of any kind.

1 There must be a plan of some kind. This may be expressed as a target, as a standard or as some other statement of what is wanted. However identified, it must be capable of being compared with what is actually happening. Usually this implies the use of some numbers, but there are many other ways of exercising effective control. This will be examined in more detail later.

2 There must be a comparison between planned performance and what is actually happening. A good example of this is the control that the captain of a ship exercises during a voyage. He sets out with a plan which consists of a port (the destination), a route, times and speeds. Continually during the voyage, he is checking to establish exactly where he is and comparing it with the plans he made at the outset. At this stage all that is going on is 'monitoring' performance.

3 The comparison has to be made often enough to ensure that any variation is identified before serious adverse effects take place. In some situations it may be only necessary to make the comparison monthly. In others continuous monitoring may be advisable.

4 Having made a comparison, the next step is to report any significant variation to the manager responsible for the activity. This implies that the responsible manager is the person in the organisation who can actually do something about the situation. It will not help the ship to arrive at the harbour by telling the cabin boy you are off course. Nor does it really help to solve the difficulty telling the sales manager's secretary that sales have dropped by forty per cent – not unless she goes and tells her boss the bad news straight away.

A key phrase to be noted here is 'significant variation'. There is little point in wasting a manager's time telling him that the sales force expenses amounted to £5,001 last week compared to an estimate of £5,000. The difference is insignificant. If, however, expenses had actually turned out at £5,200 then the manager concerned must know what has happened.

5 Speed of reporting is also essential for an effective control system. If a significant variation is found then the quicker the fact is reported to the manager concerned, the more likely something can be done to solve the difficulty. The longer the period of time between the event and the reporting, the greater the likelihood of a disaster.

6 Faced with a significant variation in performance, the wise manager will choose a suitable course of action. How quickly he does this depends on the nature of the difficulty; some things have to be dealt with instantly, other problems can best be solved if a little time is taken to think them through and discuss them

with some colleagues. There are only three possible courses of action:

- ◼ Do nothing at all. This is only recommended if the reason for the problem is a unique occurrence and is unlikely to happen again; when, for example, a thunderbolt causes a fire in a storeroom.
- ◼ Change the plan. Events occur outside the control of anyone in the organisation. If, for instance, the buyers are working to a target price for a particular raw material of £100 a kilo and a revolution in the country where the material comes from puts the price up to £150 a kilo, in that situation alternative plans must be made.
- ◼ Adjust operations. The problem may have arisen because part of the organisation is not working up to normal efficiency. The manager must identify quickly the underlying cause of the problem, then take steps to cure it. For example, if your car suddenly begins to use oil, it can be expensive to do nothing; adjustments have to be made.

7 Finally the cost of operating the control system must be justifiable. The expensive control systems in a Jumbo jet are justified on not merely cost, but because human life is involved. Most systems are concerned with costs, or quality, or safety, and always the potential loss involved should greatly exceed the cost of running the system.

Problems and benefits of control

So far we have been looking at the ingredients that are needed if anything is going to be controlled success- fully. People often talk about a 'control system', meaning a way of keeping something under control. It is possible to draw a diagram illustrating the system –

and this will apply to anything, from a large business organisation to your central heating system:

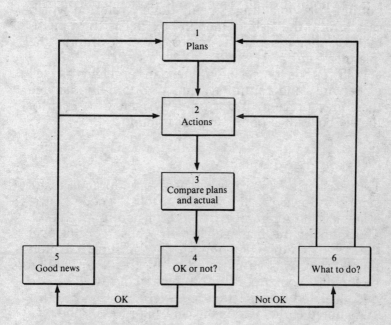

The start is the plan (box 1). This is the stage when someone in charge says, 'This is what we want to do, and this is how we are going to do it.'

This will lead to action (box 2) – the 'get on with the job' stage. Box 3 (comparing the plan with the actual events) can be summed up by the expression 'this is what we want – this is what we got'. Box 4 (OK or not?) follows box 3 closely and asks the question, 'Are we getting what we want?' If the answer is 'yes' ('OK'), then box 5 – the 'good news' box – is used. The process does not end there but runs back up to the plan box and the action box, in effect passing the message on 'What you planned and what you did have worked out well'. If the answer in box 4 is 'not OK' then box 6 is used: 'What to do?' As we saw, there are only three possibilities: either it was a freak, in which case do nothing, or something is being done wrong, in which case inform the 'action' men in box 2. The third possibility is that the plan is impossible – so inform the 'planners' in box 1.

It all sounds too easy, but there are problems as well as benefits, and control systems can do more damage than they prevent, if not properly managed. Each of the six boxes has points to bear in mind.

Plans

The existence of a plan is necessary for successful control. However, the existence of a good control system is no guarantee that the plans are any good. Think about the mad yatchsman whose control over the speed and direction of his boat were superb. Unfortunately, he was so mesmerised by the compass that he forgot to look up – and hit the harbour wall; he had miscalculated the direction to travel.

As noted earlier it aids the control process if the plan can have numbers attached to it. If we are thinking of a profit plan, then a number is automatically involved, and so are all the plans that involve revenues and costs. In some cases numbers are inappropriate: a journey plan will involve a destination; controlling the quality of a product or service may involve physical characteristics (glass bottles are visually checked for quality, no number is involved); and a newspaper editor controls the content of the paper by using some predetermined code of conduct and applying this to the stories being submitted. Again no numbers are involved, and could not be.

Actions

The actions have to be described in the same kind of way that the plans have been set. It is no use saying: 'Get this package to Mr X in Edinburgh quickly', and then complain because a plane was hired specially to carry out your instructions. So very often the actions of people have to be translated into some kind of common language which will enable the comparison to be made accurately between what happened and what ought to have happened.

All organisations keep records on the money side of their affairs, from the biggest firms in the world down to the smallest village Scout troop. It is, however, a mistake to believe that because records have been made, the requirements of good control have been met. Sometimes the records are not kept in sufficient detail to enable proper comparisons to be made. For instance, if we wanted to develop a system for controlling the costs of a fleet of lorries, control would be ineffective if nobody kept a record of the amount of fuel issued to each lorry separately – to have the fuel consumption in total is useless. Sometimes records are kept in the wrong way. Many small independent shops suffer from this problem. The accounts show all items of expenditure on overheads in great detail (rent, rates, post, telephones, etc.), but ignore the fact that the shop may be selling hundreds of different products. All that appears is one number for sales, and one number for the cost of those sales. It will not solve the problems of a firm going downhill to know precisely what the telephone bill is, if it does not know what products are selling well – and which ones make the most money.

Compare plans and actual

Earlier the question of frequency was mentioned – how often do you make the comparison? The answer depends on two things, first, the cost of making the comparison and, second, the length of time that can be allowed to elapse before a difference begins to cost an unacceptable amount (either directly in money or in some other factor like time or effort).

With food products the quality, appearance and weight have all to be of a certain standard and continuous monitoring may well be needed. The costs of carrying out the comparison are not particularly high, whereas to check the specifications in fine detail of a washing machine, for example, would be very costly; in which case there will be a degree of 'sampling' – selecting one every so often for a detailed check-up.

It will be apparent that the closer the monitoring, the less the chance of serious loss. To take the opposite view, the less frequent the comparison, the greater the chance of serious loss. But the decision has to be made, How far are you prepared to risk the possibility of a serious loss?

OK or not?

Earlier, it was suggested that the important thing to work out in answering this question was whether the difference was big enough to worry about. It was referred to as the 'significant variation' and is quite a simple idea. The problem for the manager is to decide what actually is a significant variation.

If the item to be controlled is a major factor in the firm, then a small variation will be significant. If, however, the item is of minor importance, then even a wide variation will have little impact on the firm and will not be significant.

Good news

When things are going according to plan, it is worth informing the people responsible of the good news. This does three things: it stops them worrying, it helps them resist the temptation to meddle and they feel good.

What to do

When things go adrift it was noted that only three alternative courses of action are possible: do nothing, change the plan or adjust operations. The decision depends on what caused the variation, and while it is often relatively easy to tell that something has gone adrift, it is, however, considerably more difficult to identify the real reason why things went adrift.

Information – the life and death of control

It will be plain to see that control depends on a good flow of information to the person responsible for whatever activity is being controlled. The diagram on page 195 shows various lines joining the boxes and these indicate that messages are being passed on. The lines that lead back up to the 'planning' and 'actual' boxes are called 'feedback loops' because they feed information back. This flow of information is the lifeblood of good control – without it there is no control. However, because affairs are complicated there is a tendency for information to get complicated too. For instance, a sales manager has ten salesmen reporting to him. Each sells fifteen products, each incurs expenses and is paid a commission on top of his salary. Close control of the salesmen requires the manager to look at seventeen bits of information for each salesman at least; 170 in total and a further 170 representing plans or estimates. If he has a weekly reporting system then the manager has to look at 17,680 bits of information over the year, excluding totals and cumulative figures. On top of all this there will be various statistical reports, written reports and verbal reports, all of which adds up to a huge quantity of effort and time. Yet normally only one small proportion of the activities will demand some attention. The danger for every manager is being swamped with information which may be interesting and may be relevant, but which is largely no cause for concern. Managers can be strangled by too much control information, and organisations with highly developed control systems are sometimes like the mad yachtsman we mentioned earlier.

To get round this problem, there is the technique known as 'management by exception'. With this technique, the manager simply determines what makes a significant variance, and asks to be informed of significant variances only; everything else is assumed to be OK. To be able to say 'Only tell me about the exceptional things' requires a considerable effort of will because in doing so you are trusting that people will tell you when something exceptional happens. Moreover it appears you are deliberately keeping yourself in the dark. Of course, this is not so; you are working on the principle 'no news is good news', that is, there is a plan and things are going according to plan unless you hear something.

'Management by exception' can work only if there are detailed, agreed plans. It also helps if the whole system works automatically.

Automatic controls

A good example of automatic control is in a modern home central-heating system. The thermostat is set by the home owner to a desired temperature, and from then on the system is self-regulating. If the temperature falls below the desired level then the thermostat tells the boiler to pump more heat. At the desired temperature the thermostat tells the boiler to stop pumping.

Similarly in organisations it is possible to set up ways of working where the manager need not be involved once he has 'set the thermostat'. For instance, many companies and tradesmen sell their products and services on a credit basis. In other words, at the time of sale no cash changes hands. An automatic system for collecting the money from these customers would be to instruct staff as follows:

1 Send a bill to the customer seven days after delivery of the goods.
2 After a further twenty-one days if the money has not been received send a reminder.
3 If no money is received after seven more days send a 'final reminder' (or maybe telephone the customer if his business is important).
4 Seven days later send a letter to the customer warning him of possible legal action, and send a copy to the responsible manager.

This example considerably oversimplifies how to control debtors since in reality it is often necessary to exercise discretion and be diplomatic towards one's customers. The important thing is that a way of dealing with the problem has been set which frees the manager so that he only needs to get involved if exceptional events take place; corrective action is taken automatically.

This self-correcting or self-regulating system can be built into machinery or into jobs which people do without the aid of equipment. At one extreme there are many factories where control equipment is as important and as expensive as the machinery needed to make the product itself. This is particularly true where the product is of very high value, or where its formula has to be exactly right, e.g. some chemical which could be dangerous. At the other extreme there are many control systems which are carried out entirely by people.

The computer has revolutionised the whole area of control, mainly because of its ability to deal with huge amounts of information very quickly. For instance, to have effective control over the costs in a manufacturing firm of any reasonable size and complexity requires the services of quite a few people simply to record and process quickly the information needed. The faster the information is needed, the more people have to be employed. Computers avoid this problem and are particularly useful when it comes to control by exception since the machine usually can sift faster than people.

Levels and scope of control

Just as objectives and plans can be set and made at various levels within the organisation, so too control systems are established at different levels. There has to be overall control of the organisation, to make sure that overall objectives are being met. At this level information is likely to be very different to the information a first line manager receives, although the first line manager has to keep affairs under control within the area of activity.

Similarly controls can be devised to operate on everything in an organisation: money, materials, equipment and even people. With impersonal things like money and materials the question is to decide how much control is needed to avoid significant loss. With people, an additional element is involved; it is not uncommon to have controls that identify if an individual is operating up to some expected standard – for instance, clocking in and out to make sure the hours worked are up to contract. But some systems go far beyond this, seeking to control every minute of the day. The extreme human control system was the Roman galley with its slave oarsmen. Each slave was watched over by the galley-master, and any small deviation in speed was rewarded with a lash from the whip. 'Good news' was indicated by fewer lashes.

Most managers find that they have to exercise some control over the activities of their staff; the difficulty is deciding how much control, not just over things that could result in monetary loss, but in other matters – especially how they spend their time. As we have seen, too much control leads to a feeling of not being trusted and loss of motivation. Too little control invites abuse from the idler. This problem is clearly illustrated in the 'great sales force question':

You are a sales manager with ten salesmen reporting to you. The salesmen cover a wide area of the country and you see them only on Friday afternoon when they come in to collect their expenses, receive any special instructions for the following week and review the week just past with you. Their job is to get two new customers each week. More than this and they receive a commission.

Basically, you do not know during the week what your salesmen are doing.

- Is this adequate control?
- Do you want them to phone in every day and tell you what they are doing? If so, how often each day?
- How far do the answers to the above questions depend on the kind of people your salesmen are?

If you wanted total control over your sales force, you would have them phoning in every hour from nine till five telling you where they were and what they were doing. They would do little work; you would do no work. It would be a zero sum game – a game which nobody wins. Even then you could not be entirely sure they were not sleeping or drinking between phone calls.

The extent to which control is exercised really depends on the extent to which the manager trusts his staff. If no trust exists, then control is tight; if there is a good deal of trust then controls are easier. It's worth asking the question: If there is no trust, is it a good basis to run an organisation or department?

All this is not to suggest that salesmen should not phone the office regularly. It is a feature of many companies that salesmen phone in each afternoon. The purpose is not (or should not be) control, but simply as part of an operating system – the only way to find out which customers need visiting the next day. As far as what salesmen do all day there has to be some trust – although if they are handling cash, trust should not enter into it. It is dangerous to allow much trust as far as cash and other valuables are concerned; it is asking for losses to occur.

Some important control systems

1 Budgetary control

What is a budget?

A budget is a statement which expresses somebody's plans in quantitative, usually money, terms. A sales manager may say, 'Next year I am going to put ten men on the road and they are going to bring in a lot of money.' That is his plan, but a budget will go further than that and actually identify the following things:

- How much money are the salesmen going to bring in?
- When will the sales actually be made?
- How much will the salesmen cost in terms of salaries, commission, travelling expenses, entertaining customers, etc?

Properly set up, the purposes of the budget itself are to give the manager the chance to determine for himself precisely how the part of the organisation will fare that is his responsibility. It will also give his own boss the opportunity to make sure that the kind of intentions that are being produced are in line with the overall corporate, strategic plan. Finally a budget is useful for the financial people within the organisation so that they can plan how much money to invest, or how much to borrow, at different times of the year. Individual departmental budgets form the basis, therefore, by which total operating and financial plans can be made as well as providing the individual manager with a measure of his own future performance.

Budgets are to be found in most organisations, both in the public and commercial sector, except the very small and the very inefficient. Indeed, many individuals create budgets themselves for their own private affairs by estimating income and expenditure: balancing expenditure month by month so that the amount of money in the bank never falls beyond a certain point (which may not necessarily be zero!). A budget, therefore, is the plan turned into numbers.

'Budgetary control' is the name given to the control system which uses budgets as the basis for monitoring actual performance. If the budgetary control function knows precisely what is required then it can set up the appropriate system to capture the figures and present them in the most appropriate way.

Similarly the system will not automatically come up with the basic reason for the adverse variation; it has to be deliberately built to give the information. It may look simple to be able to analyse the cause of a variance in this way and in a small, relatively uncomplicated organisation it may be so. However in large organisations, where there are many possible reasons for variances and where the sums of money involved are large, the process of diagnosis can be exceedingly complex. A good budgetary control system is one which can identify major reasons for variances *automatically* without incurring disproportionately high costs.

Other problems of budgetary control systems

Identifying the responsible manager. Everything that happens in a company is the responsibility of someone and every item of cost must be controlled by a manager. Preferably, only one manager should be responsible for a cost centre although, if there is joint responsibility, the fact must be made plain. In all cases, the manager with the budget and the responsibility must also have the power and authority to do something if things go adrift. Ultimately, in every organisation, the chief officer receives the overall variance on the budgeted profit and loss, or income and expenditure, account. This is not to say that he should see every detail and personally account for every penny of variation. He has to account for the overall result, but his subordinates have to account to him for their own spheres of responsibility. It is simply effective delegation.

Is an adverse variance always bad? The short answer is: 'No' because sometimes additional costs are incurred in making extra sales. A poorly developed budgetary control system will not allow for this, so to be sure that proper account is taken, the report that accompanies the variance statement must state:

- what happened; and
- precisely where the variances occurred.

False budgets for added protection. If a manager is asked to prepare a budget for his department he can start with a blank piece of paper and calculate what he needs to be able to perform his duties satisfactorily (sometimes known as 'zero base budgeting').

Or he can work on the basis of previous years' figures, adding a percentage to cover inflation and growth in the volume of work to be done.

If however his budget is an expenses-only budget and taken in isolation by a vetting committee, he may well decide to add on an extra twenty per cent to the total cost because previous experience indicates that the committee will prune his budget anyway.

This kind of activity is not uncommon and gives budgetary control a bad name. It is found most frequently in organisations which do not really understand the nature of the technique, where the committee is more concerned to make sure that budgets add up to a reasonable looking figure, rather than representing real plans in realistic monetary terms.

The activity is also to be found where overall expenditure limits have been set and the sum of individuals' budgets exceeds the total. This occurs frequently in government departments and local authorities when it is felt that taxes and rates cannot be raised high enough to meet spending departments' demands. Similarly in commercial organisations capital expenditure is sometimes 'rationed' if insufficient finance is available to satisfy all needs.

A completely different reason for 'padding' a budget

occurs when a manager knows that his performance will be judged by the size of the difference between the budgeted expenditure of his department and the actual amount spent. If he artificially raises his budget and gets away with it then his results will almost automatically show a favourable variance and will also hide any relatively minor inefficiencies. Clearly an undesirable system, but one which is not uncommon, occurring wherever budgetary control is imperfectly understood.

The imposed budget. Another way of setting budgets is if someone other than the person responsible does it; so instead of saying to the manager, 'What are your intentions as regards spending next year?' the question becomes a statement: 'This is what you are entitled to spend next year.' If the manager is lucky he gets more than he needs, but if he gets less than he needs he may be forced to make cuts that will spoil his department's efficiency or effectiveness.

Inflexible budgetary control. In large organisations it is not uncommon to hear people say, 'We cannot go to the lavatory unless it is in the budget', and 'The system is so tight it is strangling initiative.' Budgetary control can be a very effective system. It must however have flexibility, otherwise initiative is lost. Eventually the system runs the organisation and that can be fatal. In fact the more volatile and changeable the organisation and its environment, the greater the amount of flexibility required.

Uses of budgetary control

Since budgetary control is the way plans and actions are translated into money terms (mainly) it can be readily appreciated that this kind of system can be applied wherever the expenditure of money is involved.

The process of setting up the system can be complicated and time-consuming and the reader is referred to the many text books on management accounting to follow this aspect of the question. Suffice it to say that the system must:

- have the support of top management;
- be in tune with long-term objectives and strategies;
- be prepared early;
- involve every level of responsibility;
- be flexible;
- be understood and appreciated by all users; and
- each part must correspond with the responsibility of each manager.

This last point in effect means that each first-line manager (who has discretion regarding expenditure) will create a budget and have a control system for it, which covers his area of responsibility. Sometimes these may be referred to as 'cost centres', which technically are defined as 'a location, function or items of equipment in respect of which costs may be ascertained and related to cost units for control purposes.*

In addition, however, a budgetary control system can be devised to cover different sources of income, asset utilisation, cash and various financial activities. In fact, wherever money is involved budgetary control can be useful.

2 Standard costing

Standard costing is a technique which is similar to budgetary control in that it is concerned with providing control information about the costs of products or activi-

* *Management Accounting*, official terminology of the Institute of Cost and Management Accountants (1982).

ties. It does, however, start from a different point; whereas budgetary control compares total figures, standard costing looks at the cost of a single unit, and compares the actual cost per unit with what was expected or planned (i.e. the Standard cost of the unit).

The actual cost is obtained from accounting records; the standard cost is based on individual managers' estimates (budgets). The system is used particularly to identify variances in the buying price of materials or in the usage of materials (it is an excellent way of identifying quickly an unacceptable level of wastage). It is also in use for controlling labour costs where there are predetermined standards of labour time and money for jobs.

3 Quality control

It is one thing to be able to control the cost of a product and the quantity of materials used in making it; it is however a completely different type of control to make sure that the product is of precisely the quality that has been planned. Quality may not reach a predetermined standard for a number of reasons:

- the product may be underweight;
- it may be misformed or wrongly coloured;
- it may not be up to the correct specifications or formula;
- it may contain (in food and drink) a 'foreign body';
- it may be damaged;
- it may smell incorrect.

Quality can go wrong in many different places. The commonest are:

- at the point of delivery;
- in storage (e.g. due to deterioration);

- throughout the production process;
- in packing;
- in transit to the customer.

Each potential *location* of a quality defect and each potential *type* of defect have to be the concern of the quality control staff. In some instances the adage that prevention is better than cure is appropriate. Hence the use of screens to keep out flies in food factories. A good quality control system will be one which draws up its specifications, plans and procedures carefully so that the risk of defective products is reduced.

A 100 per cent guarantee of no defects cannot be made, but as we indicated earlier if the product is medical or for consumption, or is high-technology or potentially dangerous, then quality controls will be much more stringent than in low-value, harmless products. Also quality controls will be tougher where a product has a quality image.

Random spot-checking

Random spot-checks are used if there is a limited amount of money available for quality control. Before such a system is introduced, however, everyone involved must be made aware of what is going to happen. Nothing is more likely to cause trouble than a sudden visit from a quality control inspector unannounced, unexpected and for the first time. It is better still if groups are made responsible for their own quality control.

A quality control problem

It is useful to bear in mind with the quality control of finished products that testing and inspection can take as long as actual production – or longer with sophisticated electronics. Until a product is given that final OK it is not ready for sale but is still work-in-progress and a drain on the resources of the business, locking up expensive capital. When there is a possibility of this occurring, the inspection and testing function has to be given high priority in the allocation of human and equipment resources.

4 Stock control

Some of the problems associated with control of stocks have been mentioned in Chapter 8 in relation to rules about buying. With stock control the problems can be identified as:

- Running out of space.
- Having items in the wrong place.
- Running short of key items.
- Having an excess of useless items.
- Losing items (through pilferage, animal pests or deterioration).

All the problems can relate to raw materials, components, packaging, sub-assemblies and finished goods, but whichever problem occurs, money is lost. Stock control systems have to minimise the loss.

Effective stock control can be achieved if it is built into a standard costing system, if it is related to control of the buying function (prevention of speculative buying is important here) and also related to quality control.

The importance of an effective stock control system is that every organisation has only a limited amount of money. If it is being spent on materials and in production at a faster rate than it is coming in from sales, sooner or later there is a cash crisis. This is known as the working capital problem, or the cash flow crisis, and often arises because of overenthusiastic buying ('fantastic bargain') or piling up finished goods ('there's a boom time just around the corner').

5 Computer-based systems

The advent of computers resulted in a very fast growth of control systems using all the advantages of rapid processing and storage of data. Much of this growth occurred in larger organisations which felt that the costs could be justified in terms of the potential savings that could result.

Nowadays, with the coming of microcomputers and the widespread use of computer service bureaux, there is the real opportunity for even the smallest organisation to have control systems that would have been impossibly expensive in 1960, or even 1970. Computer-based information or control systems can provide effective answers to many of the problems facing the small firm, but it has to be kept clearly in mind that their use is only successful if the plans which are being controlled are good.

6 Overall control

Overall control of an organisation takes place in the same way that different parts of an organisation are controlled. This is achieved by comparing overall performance with plans, usually via such reports as the trading accounts, profit and loss accounts and balance sheets. These traditional accounting statements do not of themselves monitor progress, but if they are related to corporate budgets, variances in total performance can be quickly identified.

Every organisation needs good control systems – not

so that employees can be rewarded or punished (a common mistake) but so that the chances of going on the rocks are reduced to a minimum.

Beware the silly system

Finally on control, one other thing to guard against is the 'silly system'. This is a system designed to do a job which becomes a monster – helping nobody and irritating everyone. A crazy example is the company that decided to control its salesforce by limiting the petrol put into their car tanks.

Every morning each salesman completed a form (four parts) on which he had to state the number of miles he intended to travel. This was countersigned by his boss and then taken to the controller's office who would check it and approve it. The salesman would then take the form and his car to the petrol pump and have the appropriate gallons put into the tank (according to the number of miles he was forecasting). At the end of the day his mileage was checked and the petrol in the tank was also checked by means of a dipstick. The form was then completed and the various parts distributed (together with various statistical analyses) at the end of the week to all concerned.

Crazy? Silly? Maybe – but every organisation has got a system somewhere inside it that is not far off being as silly as this. Controls, therefore, can help an organisation achieve its objectives, but too much emphasis on control can stifle initiative and lead to lack of motivation, and too much control can cost more than it saves. A good system of control needs a lot of different features to make it work properly, but in the end the best control system in the world is no good if the plans being controlled are no good.

12 The Successful Business: The Management Task

Most managers would rather work for, and in, a successful firm than in an unsuccessful one. There are exceptions, of course, where the manager takes on a job in a poor company because he believes he can turn it round and because he enjoys a challenge. Sir Michael Edwardes' stint at BL comes into this category. For the most part though, managers want to be associated with success, not failure; success provides material and psychological rewards.

The questions that need to be answered now are:

- What is a successful business?
- What must the manager do to create success?

The successful business

A successful firm provides a reasonable reward to its main stakeholders over a long period of time: the main stakeholders being the owners of the business and the employees. In a very small firm, the owners are the employees as well and their criterion of success will be that the business gives them a comfortable living, with capital growth, in the long-run. Where ownership and management are split, the owners or shareholders – will expect dividend growth and an increase in the value of their shares. Employees will expect good pay increases, fringe benefits, a bonus scheme and, increasingly, a share-option scheme for managers. Many employees will also expect good promotion prospects and opportunities.

In all cases, growth and rising expectations seem to figure large, though it is open to debate how big the growth has to be if the firm is to be described as 'successful' – presumably the increases will be better than average.

There are two underlying factors in determining a firm's degree of success, namely its *Present status* and its *Prospects* (or *Expectations*). In other words, how is it doing now and what are its chances of doing well in the future?

How to judge a firm's present status

To assess whether a firm is currently successful, several features need to be studied. These include:

- Has the firm achieved substantial growth over the last five years in profits, sales, assets employed and in its equity capital base?
- Has there been a better than average increase in dividend payments in recent years?
- Is the company generating a positive cash-flow?
- How profitable is the firm, measured by return on capital employed, or return on equity?
- Is the company financially sound and not likely to become insolvent (i.e. unable to pay its debts)?
- What do people think of the company?

How to judge a firm's prospects

- What line(s) of business is it in? (There are not many prospects for a firm making radio-valves, nor for one making bowler hats). The markets that the firm is serving must have growth potential.

- Are the products or services being offered attractive to the customers? In other words, is there likely to be a reasonable demand and has the company identified and exploited some 'market niches' where it can dominate a market and be a leader?
- Is the company a leader in its own technologies?
- Does the company have a creative, energetic and able top management team?
- How good is its industrial relations record?
- Has it acquired any new business recently, or disposed of any old business?
- In the case of a public company, how does the stockmarket rate it? A high share price usually indicates that investors believe the firm has good prospects.

These questions are indicators of how success can be judged and provide clues to the second question: What must the manager do to create success?

Business success: the manager's job

Very simply, a business will fail for one of two possible reasons. Either it fails to sell enough of its products or services, at a good enough price, to cover its costs and the investment that has been made in the firm. Or, it is so inefficient that it fails to make enough profit or generate enough cash to be able to keep going.

In either case, management has failed. Plenty has been written about how to avoid business failure and how to achieve success. Here are a few important rules, covering each of the two aspects defined above:

Selling enough

- Remember 'the marketing mix' –
  Make sure there is a demand for the product, make sure the price is sensible, get the product in the right market and make sure the customers know about it (and can obtain it!)
- At the end of the day, it is the customer who decides if you sell anything: look after the customers, find out what they want, listen to them, respond to their needs and try to anticipate their needs in the future.
- Make sure that everyone in the company realises how important customers are. And so: 1. treats each one accordingly. 2. makes sure that the product (or service) is first class, with no defects or cause for complaint.
- Train everyone who sells, or who has customer contact, so they are familiar with all aspects of the product or service and can discuss it with enthusiasm and pride.

Be efficient

- Set up sensible purchasing policies and buy carefully.
- Choose an operating system which concentrates on getting the job done fast, at least cost. This includes raising productivity. Note that this does not mean working harder; it means working more effectively.
- Keep tight control over money, especially working capital items: stock levels and debtors.
- It must be possible to justify every £1 spent on overheads. If you can't, don't spend it.
- All systems must help managers; if they do not, get new ones.
- Utilise all assets as fully as possible. A piece of

equipment only used once a month is not earning its keep.

The role of planning

The job of management is to make sure that all the factors that can influence success are taken account of. To be able to do this, managers must PLAN; indeed if there is one feature above all others which distinguishes good firms from poor firms, it is the extent to which the managers are planners. There are, of course, always plenty of reasons for not planning – one of the commonest being: 'There isn't enough time; we're too busy fire-fighting'. This is not really a reason; it is more of an excuse, the point being that good planning gives managers more time to concentrate on developing the business and often prevents crises happening.

More than seventy years ago, Henri Fayol wrote of the importance of planning, and said that failure to plan signifies managerial incompetence . . .

A few years before, F. W. Taylor was worrying about inefficient management and asserting that a systematic approach to business, including planning, would provide the remedy. He wrote that if the principles of scientific management were followed, the results would be 'truly astounding'.

Another classic writer on management, Chester Barnard, said some fifty years ago that one of the most important tasks of management is decision-taking, and that getting the timing right is all-important. In business the most important decisions are about the future. If not enough time is allowed for proper analysis of the problem, or for a proper evaluation of all the options, the manager ends up with no options . . . he is no longer master of his own destiny.

Since the time of these three great management thinkers, a mass of literature has been published to confirm the importance of planning. Success is the result of hard planning and thinking about the future; 'think until it hurts' was Lord Thomson's formula for business success.

Whose responsibility?

In a small firm, the owner will most likely be the chief executive, if not the only manager in the business. The danger is to become bogged down in day to day matters, leaving no time for thinking and planning. The way out of the trap is to delegate as much of the routine work as possible, no matter how enjoyable it is. If you are the boss, you are not there to do the routine tasks that anyone can do.

This principle applies to all managers – delegate as much as you can to give yourself thinking time.

In a large company, all managers have a contribution to make in securing the firm's success. Clearly, only top management is in a position to determine the grand strategy of the entire corporation. However, within that, each division, sub-company and department needs to have its own plans, its own policies, systems and structures. Top management should delegate responsibility for determining all these matters to the managers who will have to carry out the job (subject to overall corporate strategies and policies).

Finally, a poor business is one where either the management is wrong, or it is the wrong kind of business to be in. A successful firm is in the right kind of business and has the right management. But remember, success today does not guarantee success tomorrow and never trust to luck.

Further Reading

Peter F Drucker, *Management* (Pan Books, 1979)

Igor H Ansoff, *Corporate Strategy* (Penguin, 1968)

R. Wild, *Production and Operations Management – Principles and Techniques* (Holt, Rinehart and Winston, 1979)

Roger Oldcorn, *Company Accounts* (Pan Books, 1986)

John Fawn and Bernard Cox (eds), *Corporate planning in practice* (Institute of Cost and Management Accountants, 1985)

Michael Porter, *Competitive Strategy: techniques for analysing industries and competitors* (Collier Macmillan, 1980)

Thomas J. Peters and Robert H. Waterman, *In Search of Excellence* (Harper and Row, 1982)

The review of the Boston Consulting Group's techniques was in *The Financial Times*, 11, 13, 16 November 1981.

To keep up to date, read *Management Today, Harvard Business Review, Fortune* and *The Financial Times*.

Index

Peter F. Drucker
Management £3.95

Peter Drucker's aim in this major book is 'to prepare today's and tomorrow's managers for performance'. He presents his philosophy of management, refined as a craft with specific skills: decision making, communication, control and measurement, analysis – skills essential for effective and responsible management in the late twentieth century.

'Crisp, often arresting . . . A host of stories and case histories from Sears Roebuck, Marks and Spencer, IBM, Siemens, Mitsubishi and other modern giants lend colour and credibility to the points he makes' ECONOMIST

The Practice of Management £3.95

'Peter Drucker has three outstanding gifts as a writer on business – acute perception, brilliant skill as a reporter and unlimited self-confidence . . . his penetrating accounts of the Ford Company . . . Sears Roebuck . . . IBM . . . are worth a library of formal business histories' NEW STATESMAN

'Those who now manage ought to read it: those who try to teach management ought to buy it' TIMES EDUCATIONAL SUPPLEMENT

Managing for Results £2.95

'A guide to do-it-yourself management . . . contains first-class suggestions that have the great virtue that they are likely to be widely and easily applicable to almost every business' TIMES REVIEW OF INDUSTRY

'Excellent . . . well-supported examples of what has happened in practice to companies that have thought in this analytical way' FINANCIAL TIMES